Technology Tips for Seniors

JEFFREY ALLEN AND ASHLEY HALLENE

AMERICAN BAR ASSOCIATION
Senior Lawyers
Division

Cover design by Jill Tedhams/ABA Design

The materials contained herein represent the opinions of the authors and/or the editors, and should not be construed to be the views or opinions of the law firms or companies with whom such persons are in partnership with, associated with, or employed by, nor of the American Bar Association or the Senior Lawyers Division unless adopted pursuant to the bylaws of the Association.

Nothing contained in this book is to be considered as the rendering of legal advice for specific cases, and readers are responsible for obtaining such advice from their own legal counsel. This book is intended for educational and informational purposes only.

© 2016 American Bar Association. All rights reserved.

No part of this publication may be reproduced, stored in a retrieval system, or transmitted in any form or by any means, electronic, mechanical, photocopying, recording, or otherwise, without the prior written permission of the publisher. For permission contact the ABA Copyrights & Contracts Department, copyright@americanbar.org, or complete the online form at http://www.americanbar.org/utility/reprint.html.

Printed in the United States of America.

20 19 18 17   5 4

Library of Congress Cataloging-in-Publication Data

Names: Allen, Jeffrey (Jeffrey Michael), author. | Hallene, Ashley, author.
Title: Technology tips for seniors / by Jeffrey Allen and Ashley Hallene.
Description: First edition. | Chicago : American Bar Association, 2016.
Identifiers: LCCN 2016019610 | ISBN 9781634255240 (print : alk. paper)
Subjects: LCSH: Computers and older people. | Internet and older people. |
    Technology and older people.
Classification: LCC QA76.9.O43 A45 2016 | DDC 004.084/6—dc23
LC record available at https://lccn.loc.gov/2016019610

Discounts are available for books ordered in bulk. Special consideration is given to state bars, CLE programs, and other bar-related organizations. Inquire at Book Publishing, ABA Publishing, American Bar Association, 321 N. Clark Street, Chicago, Illinois 60654-7598.

www.ShopABA.org

R0452316532

Table of Contents

Tips to Protect Your Privacy and Identity 167

Introduction

The importance of technology in our professional and personal lives has grown more dramatically during the lives of those of us over age 65 than any other generation in history. It continues to grow at an ever-increasing rate. Those of us still practicing law must deal with technology in our professional lives, as clients demand the availability that the Internet, e-mail, and mobile devices provide, and many courts have moved to a requirement of electronic filing and communications with the court.

The profession has moved toward recognizing a duty for attorneys to acquire a level of basic competence in dealing with technology. The ABA model rules have recognized that duty. More and more state bars are coming to the same conclusion.

Technology can help lawyers practice more efficiently and effectively. As a result, attorneys of all ages have grown increasingly interested in learning about technology. Some of the more senior attorneys have adopted an ostrich-like approach to technology, operating under the theory that if they don't use it, they do not have to understand it. That head-in-the-sand approach won't work much longer (to the extent that it ever did), as we approach the point of concluding that a lawyer's failure to make appropriate use of available technology can constitute an ethical breach.

For those of us who have stopped practicing law (or are in the process of doing that), technology offers us the opportunity to continue to grow and learn at a rapid rate. It also offers us the ability to take care of mundane chores (like shopping) easily, quickly, and efficiently, without leaving our home or office. Learning about technology may prevent our children or grandchildren from saying "Grandma [or Grandpa], you don't know anything about technology" (as one grandmother recently reported that her 12-year-old granddaughter recently told her).

Perhaps even more importantly, learning about technology can make it easier for us to communicate with our children and grandchildren, or with the many friends we have made over the years through our associations with the ABA and other organizations, located in other cities or states (or even countries).

We have done programs presenting tips on technology and practice for many years in locations all over the country. We have also written about technology for lawyers for many years. We often get questions about our tips programs. Sometimes the questions come from people who attended or read an article but want additional information. Many times we get questions from those who could not attend a show, asking about topics we covered or requesting copies of the slide show.

We thoroughly enjoy doing those programs and writing those articles. We were delighted when the SLD asked us to create this book for the division. The purpose is to highlight some of the most popular and important tips we have addressed in our programs, with a focus on making them "senior-friendly" and to augment those tips with some that we felt would particularly interest seniors. We were even more pleased when they told us that they would like us to prepare a new edition of the book every year or so covering the new material we brought into our programs and new technology that comes onto the market.

As we prepared this book, we realized that many younger attorneys (and many nonlawyers) would benefit from the tips and suggestions offered here, just as seniors can benefit from the tips and suggestions that we have offered in other books that we did not write with a focus on senior readers. In part, that comes from recognizing that the perception that seniors suffer from technological challenges is largely a misperception. The simple fact of the matter is that this generation of seniors learned to adapt to more and greater changes in technology than any other generation in recorded history. We see no reason that as seniors we should not reflect that same adaptability that saw us through the evolution from ballpoint pens (or even fountain pens) and paper to the manual and then the electric typewriter to the computer, from carbon paper to the photocopy machine, from snail mail to e-mail, and from nothing through the VHS and Beta wars to digital video recordings.

We have tried to present the tips in this book as we would in a program. We do not go into great detail as to any of the tips or recommendations. We present them briefly to introduce the information or the product to you for further investigation or consideration. We anticipate that some of you may have heard or read some of the tips before, perhaps at one of our presentations or in one of our articles. We expect that many of you will find much of the information in this book new to you. We also anticipate that many of the tips in this book will prove useful to most attorneys either in their professional lives or their personal lives or both.

We have tried to make this book more senior-friendly by avoiding as much as possible the use of jargon (aka "technotalk", aka "geekspeak") and by using simple grammatical English to address the concepts we discuss in this book. We have also asked the ABA to instruct the publisher to use a larger font so that seniors will find the book more easily read. We hope this approach resonates with you.

We hope that you will enjoy this book and the style of presentation we use for the tips. We anticipate that the book will be the start of a relationship with many readers who will look forward to each new edition of the book, to see what new information they can get, what new technology we have learned about, and what new software and hardware might prove useful to them. For many others, it will continue an already existing relationship that we have with you through our programs and other writings.

We hope that you will find some tips in this book and in our future editions that will help you in your professional and your personal lives by making things easier for you to accomplish, making you more efficient or more effective as an attorney, or making your life a little bit easier or more enjoyable. Please note that while we have endeavored to organize the tips into logical groupings in each chapter, there will inevitably be some overlap because some tips fit in more than one category. We have imposed the following organization on the tips we have collected for you in this book:

1. Tips for using mobile devices
2. Tips for using your computer
3. Tips for using the Internet to communicate with friends and family
4. Tips for sharing media with friends and family
5. Tips for travel
6. Tips to protect your privacy and identity
7. Health and technology (including apps to keep your brain tuned up)
8. Miscellaneous

A Word about the Authors

Jeffrey Allen has practiced law for over 40 years and belonged to the Senior Lawyers' Division of the American Bar Association for over 17 years. He has learned from experience what it means to get older. He grew up long before Al Gore created the Internet (for those of you who believe that he actually invented it, the language he used in the interview specifically did not say "invent"; his exact language was: "I took the initiative in creating the Internet"). Ashley Hallene, on the other hand (we call her the "Whippersnapper"), has just reached 32 years (in age, not years of practice). She still belongs to the Young Lawyers' Division. Jeff and Ashley have worked together for the past few years and written several books and articles together. The pair brings you a perspective that spans time and experience, giving you input from one who grew up in the age of the Internet and one who grew up in the period when every house did not even have a television set yet (and those that did had small-screen black-and-white TVs).

Tips for Using Your Mobile Devices

Although we can consider laptops and other devices as "mobile devices," in this section we focus on mobile phones and tablets, including the new cross between the two that has acquired the moniker "phablet," thus bridging the name as well as the technology.

We often get questions about what phone or tablet to buy. Consequently, we regularly check out new phones and tablets so that we can write and talk about them. We do not claim that we have checked out every phone and every tablet that has come on to the market, however. We have not tried to do that, as the task would prove insurmountable and some manufacturers have not been inclined to provide us with review units.

Through our efforts, however, we have found hardware that we think works well and can prove useful to attorneys and have identified some of that hardware for you in the tips included in this book and in our other articles and programs.

We do not suggest that other pieces of hardware may not work as well for you as those we discuss, nor do we suggest that you may not prefer different hardware. What we talk about in this section works for us and impressed us as useful. Even if you do not decide to get hardware we talk about in this section, we think you will find this information useful. If nothing else, it should give you a place to start looking and something to use as a standard for the comparison of hardware in which you may be interested.

Remember that hardware manufacturers survive on making and selling new products. Sometimes a manufacturer makes substantial and substantive changes in the newer models; sometimes a new model makes only some cosmetic changes. Occasionally, a newer model does not work as well or reliably as its predecessor. You should not assume that just because the manufacturer offers a newer model of the hardware we talk about that the newer model will work better or that you should run out and buy one. You should also take note of the fact that when a new model comes out, you can often pick up the previous model at a substantial discount. This savings can more than make up for not having the additional features offered with the new model.

Be a smart buyer; in deciding whether to pay the cost of the new model to get the additional features or take the discount and get the older model, compare the features of the new model to the older one and then look at the price differential. If the new features do not help you, then you do not need them. If the cost of the new features does not appear to justify what they add, you are well advised to get the older model and save the money. On the other hand, if they make the product significantly better, they may well justify their cost. Recognize that "better," like "beauty," lies in the beholder's eye. You should analyze in terms of whether the new features improve the device for you, not in some absolute value sense of quality.

If you do not get a substantial discount for the older model and the new model appears at least as good as the older one, you will likely do better getting the new model.

In this section, we give you some more advice about what to get and how to purchase your device and to feed it connectivity. We also suggest a number of applications, or apps, available to you to expand the utility and functionality of your phone, tablet, and/or phablet (a word used to reference large-display phones, such as the iPhone 6/6S Plus and the Galaxy Note 4), and provide some information about how to use them effectively. Software (aka apps) makes our computers, smartphones, and tablets do most of what they do for us. Without software, the smartphones would not act so smart, and tablets would, largely, be expensive media display devices. A good selection of software will help you get the most value and functionality from your mobile devices. Speaking of software, we have highlighted certain apps in other sections of this book for you. Be sure to check them out; we think you will want to add most, if not all, of them to your devices.

For smartphones and tablets, the best source of software or apps is the store set up for distribution of such software by the developer of the hardware operating system. The operating system, or "OS," is the basic set of instructions that tells the device how to behave.

The two best-known providers of hardware operating systems for mobile devices are Google (Android) and Apple (iOS). Google's Play Store (Seriously? We still cannot get over what a poor choice of names that proved) distributes software from Google and from other developers compatible with the Android operating system. Apple's iTunes Store has an Apps section to distribute its own apps and those from other developers. While developers of other operating systems have established their own software app venue, none of the others compares favorably with Google's Play Store, and we don't think that Google's Play Store favorably compares to Apple's iTunes App Store in terms of the range or quantity of available apps.

When you are dealing with smartphones and tablets, it is often difficult to add software to the device except through purchase at the appropriate distribution center (the iTunes App Store or Google Play Store). You have an additional advantage in getting software from the operating system developer's software store in that the developer does check out the software prior to adding it to the store, so you get a bit of protection that way.

We make no apology for the fact that both of us prefer the Apple iOS to the other available systems, and we have used iPads and iPhones extensively. While we have worked with other devices to test them, we keep coming back to the iOS platform. We also talk a bit about what we think of as the "Second System"—the Android OS and its Google Play Store (for your online media and software shopping pleasure). If you do not already know it, apps written for the iOS will not work on Android devices and apps written for the Android OS will not work on iOS devices. You can pretty much use the same media on both types of devices, but some media will be locked to one system or another.

Get a Smartphone and a Tablet

We believe that, as a practical matter, most people should have both smartphones and tablets. Yes, for some that will be overkill; but for most, the two will serve you well together. We make this suggestion for several reasons:

- While some of the same software runs on smartphones and tablets, some software runs only on a phone and other software runs only on a tablet. Having both increases flexibility.
- You can do voice chats on both smartphones and tablets, but smartphones do much better at making voice communications available to you (after all, they are telephones).
- Smartphones are more portable, so that you will likely take them everywhere (probably best not to include the shower or swimming pool though [unless you cleverly got a waterproof case first]).
- Smartphones (even the phablet sizes) have far smaller displays than most

tablets. The smaller display may make the device more portable, but the larger display makes it easier to see and to work (an increasingly important consideration for seniors, particularly as we grow more and more senior).

- Watching a video or a movie (or for that matter, viewing a still photo of your grand-children or your last vacation trip) will prove more pleasant and satisfying on a tablet due to its larger display.
- Tablets generally have more powerful processors and can do more and do it more quickly than smartphones. For many users, the tablet can functionally replace a laptop.

Choose the Proper Equipment for Your Situation

Some people will find that one operating system suits them better than another. Most will find that they prefer certain hardware over other hardware. Many will find their choice of hardware restricted by the service provider they choose to use. Almost all mobile devices are OS (operating system) specific. Some are provider specific as well. For example, when Apple introduced the iPad, the company locked it into AT&T. That has changed now and you can get an iPad that will work with most providers and certainly all of the major providers. Some manufacturers create different models for different providers. The different models generally reflect some minor feature and cosmetic differences.

Before you buy any mobile device, consider where you will use it (geographically). Check coverage maps (available online) to see what providers offer the best and most comprehensive coverage in your geographical area(s). In almost all cases, that will be the provider you want to use (even if it costs a bit more, because the savings in cost generally never equal the price in frustration if your carrier keeps dropping calls). Once you have decided on your provider, make sure you choose equipment that works with that provider. While making that consideration, note that the newest and fastest service is generally referred to as "4G," which stands for fourth generation. For most providers in most locations, 4G is replacing its predecessor (cleverly known as "3G"). When you check your coverage maps, look for clarity as to which areas get 4G and which get 3G. Most of the newer phones default to 4G but also work on 3G when they cannot find 4G availability. Adoption of 4G started in primarily densely populated urban areas and has branched out from there. Rural areas will most likely have only 3G service available for a while.

Smartphones and tablets can do all kinds of things. Decide what you think you will do with them and give some thought to what you would like to learn to do with them before you buy. Then look for devices that best do the things you want to do. Now that you have a (hopefully relatively short) list of potential devices, look at the features of each and decide whether one looks like it will work best for you. Using that approach should get you down to a very few devices. Pick the one you like best overall (here is where cosmetics come into play), and you should be good to go.

Memory also can become an issue (not yours; your device's memory). The amount of memory the device has dictates how much you can add to it in the form of media and software. The lower the memory, the less you can add. The less you can add, the less useful the device becomes. iOS devices come with memory that you cannot supplement, except by external devices. What you buy is what you get, and you keep that for as long as you have the device. Yes, you can swap content and move some off and more onto the device, but doing that can be bothersome and we try to avoid having to do that very much. Many Android devices will accept Micro SD cards to allow you to augment the memory that comes with the device. While that does make things better, it does not entirely solve the problem. The ability to augment the memory with an SD card allows you to add content to the card and use it with the device; however, many programs cannot run from the SD card and have to be in the device's fixed memory to run (some run just fine from the card). If you have limited memory, you have to be choosier about what you put on the device or plan on regularly moving things on and off it. For that reason, we like to get larger memory rather than smaller. We balk at Android devices of less than 32 GB and will not get one with less than 16 GB. On the iOS side, we balk at less than 64 GB and won't drop below 32 GB. Because the cost of the additional memory has dropped, we prefer the 128 GB iOS devices. Apple has just made a 256 GB 9.7" iPad Pro available. We welcome that increase, but for many it will prove more than you need. For most users, we like the 128 GB size. If you plan to add a lot of media to your device and you go with Apple, you may want to consider the 256 GB size. Now that Apple has offered the 256 GB in one iPad, expect it to offer that size memory in other devices.

You can often get discounts on mobile devices from service providers by committing yourself to a contract with that provider for a year or two.

We have already disclosed our predisposition for iOS products. We do not mean to disparage Android products because we think that Android is the best system out there (except for iOS). In truth, we have played with Android phones and tablets and have, as a general rule, liked them. The real difference is the fact that we consider the iTunes App Store as superior to Google's Play Store.

When it comes to Android devices, our favorites come from Samsung, and we have particularly liked the Note and Galaxy S series of phones. In fact, if you look at the hardware specifications of the top end of the Samsung smartphones, phablets, and tablets, they often equal or exceed those of Apple's iPhone and iPad.

Let Your Devices Be All That They Can Be

Tablets and smartphones with appropriate software can do an amazing collection of tasks for us. Here's a partial list.

Some of The AMAZING Things a Tablet or Smartphone Can Do

Serve as a calendar	Keep track of contacts	Handle "to-dos" and reminders
Enable you to videoconference	Take digital still photographs	Edit digital still photographs
Display digital still photographs	Record videos	Edit videos
Play videos	Function as a notepad	Function as a diary
Play audio and visual media	Function as an e-reader	Function as an educational device
Function as a calculator	Function as a currency converter	Function as a medical device
Track activities	Track caloric intake	Function as a fax machine
Function as an e-mail appliance	Surf the Internet	Work as a photo album

(*Continued*)

Some of The AMAZING Things a Tablet or Smartphone Can Do (*Continued*)

Work as an electronic photo display appliance	Translate to and from other languages	Handle banking transactions
Serve as a digital wallet	Keep financial records	Store database information
Stream content from the Internet	Help create and edit documents	Help with shopping
Serve as a research tool (legal and other research)	Act as a bookkeeping device	Provide time and billing services
Play games	Function as a digital assistant	Send and receive SMS (short text) messages
Keep track of travel information	Record music	Write music
Play music	Provide world time	Provide weather information for cities near and far
Act as a concierge	Act as a travel guide	Help make appropriate travel arrangements

(Continued)

Some of The AMAZING Things a Tablet or Smartphone Can Do (*Continued*)

Navigate for you on foot and in or on vehicles	Function as a medical record storing device	Function as a cellular Wi-Fi hotspot
Function as a remote control device	Function as a home and vehicle monitoring device	Function as a babysitter (well sort of; it can sure keep a grandchild occupied happily for a prolonged period of time)

The list goes on and on and on, potentially endlessly. Just remember that whatever it is or may become, there is an app for that (or there will likely be one soon).

Password-Protect Your Devices

We do not know of any current smartphone or tablet that does not offer you the ability to password-protect access to your device. Many of the newer devices also include biometric access protection (generally used in conjunction with a password) in the form of a fingerprint scanner. Once you get a new device and connect it to your provider, you should immediately set up password (and fingerprint if available) protection for your device.

Some devices let you draw a design on the display and use that for access. We generally don't like that approach, as we have found the process either too restrictive or not restrictive enough. A large number of devices default to a four-digit passcode (some have recently upped that to a six-digit passcode). Most devices also allow you to opt for a more detailed and longer password. We recommend that you do that and that you choose an alphanumeric password, preferably one that uses both capital and lowercase letters. If your device allows it, adding symbolic characters ups the ante in terms of protection. Pick something that has a meaning for you, so that you can remember it. For example, if you were a Michael Jordan fan, you might choose "mICHAEL23" or, even better, "!mICHAEL23!". Do note, however that if you have an obsession with Michael Jordan, that password would probably be a relatively easy guess by someone who knows you. In that case, you might want to stay away from derivatives of his name. On the other hand, if you liked Joe DiMaggio a lot, you could always go with "$MrCoffeeNYY5" (for those who were not fans, Joe DiMaggio did a lot of work for the Mr. Coffee people and wore number 5 when he played for the New York Yankees [NYY]). Anyway, you get the idea: choose something that people who know you won't easily identify (such as your name or initials), modify it in terms of case, and add some numbers and symbols. If your device uses a biometric scanner for access, you won't have to use the password often, making a longer and more secure password less onerous.

Set Up Your Calendar and Contacts

You will want to set up your calendar information and your contacts on your mobile devices, and you will want the devices to synchronize with each other so that you have to make a change only one time for it to get to both of your devices. Both the iOS and Android devices can handle that task well and reliably.

Both Android and iOS devices come with preinstalled programs that can handle those tasks, but you may want to use something that works a bit differently than what comes with the system. You can find a large selection of software in this category at Apple's iTunes Store and Google's Play Store. If you are still in practice, many practice management programs can link to, accept entries from, and update data to your mobile devices.

We like to keep things relatively simple and have found that, at least for our work, Apple's Calendar and Contacts apps work quite well on the iOS platform. We have found that those apps do everything we need to do in a solo or small firm practice. In a larger firm, they will likely fall a bit short, so you might want to use a different program, particularly if your firm already has a practice management program in place and it works with mobile devices. It is worth noting that, while you can work from iOS versions of Calendar and Contacts and coordinate with Windows-based computers and/or Android mobile devices, the procedure leaves something to be desired. As a general rule, we have found that the iOS apps work best with Mac OS computers using the same apps for the computer and synching through iCloud (Apple's cloud-based storage and synchronization). Conversely, Android software generally works best with Windows-based computers and programs. We have had some issues synching between Android apps and iOS and Mac OS devices and software. We have also had some issues with Google Calendar and iOS synching.

For you Outlook users, you can use Outlook on iOS and Android as well as Mac OS and Windows platforms.

If you have previously worked on one or the other systems, switching over does not present a major problem. It is worth the time, however, to print out a copy of your contacts and calendar and spend a bit of time proofing to make sure that all the data moved appropriately.

When you set up your calendar, you might want to set up more than one for yourself. That way, you can share some information and keep other information private. For example, if your children like to know when you are out of town so that they can make other baby-sitting arrangements for your grandchildren, you can set up a travel calendar and enter information only about out-of-town trips on it. By sharing that calendar with your children and moving other information to different, unshared calendars, you can give them what they need without bothering them with other things that do not concern them (such as professional meetings), local social events, and so on. Similarly, you can have a professional and a personal calendar, sharing the latter with your friends or your spouse (or a functional equivalent) and the former with your secretary, paralegal, and so on.

Make sure you set up your devices to sync to the same account (usually through a cloud-based server) to enable you to automatically update all your devices whenever you make a change on one of them. Remember, however, that your device will not upgrade unless you have it online. If you turn off your device, it will need some time to connect and update after you turn it back on and it connects to the Internet.

Smartphone, Come Home!

Who among us has not misplaced their smartphone or their tablet (or both)? OK, to put it another way, we can divide everyone who reads this section into two groups: those who have misplaced their smartphone and/or tablet and those who will misplace their smartphone and/or tablet. By the way, in case you worry about such things, misplacing your smartphone does not reflect dementia, Alzheimer's, or senility. Plenty of 20- and 30-somethings have done it and will do it. The biggest difference between them and the 60- and 70- and 80-somethings who do it is that the younger-somethings don't worry so much about what it means. Anyway, as luck would have it, there's an app for that!

If you use the iOS system, turn on the Find My iPhone feature. Bonus! It also works on iPads. Set it up and link it to your iCloud account, and you are good to go. Just be sure you leave your device turned on and airplane mode turned off. The device needs to connect to the Internet to let you find it. Once you have it set up and it has connected to the Internet, you can locate it (at least its general vicinity) using another iOS device or a computer with an Internet connection. The app can tell you pretty much where you left the device (the app can get you to a building but not the suite or room number, so you have to remember where you were in that building by yourself). You can also have it beep to help you locate it when you are close to it. For example, if the app tells you that you left the phone in your office building, you can probably figure out where your office is, but that doesn't tell you where the device is in the office. If you left it sitting on your desk, you may see it easily and that solves the problem. Often, however, the reason you forgot the device is that you cleverly put something over it and hid it from view. Here is where the audio tone comes into play. If you hear the tone and determine it is somewhere on your desk, you can move things around until you find it. Without that capability, you could look for a long time without finding it.

If you have an Android device, you do not have to feel left out. Google's Play

Store has a Find My Android Phone app for you, too.

A related trick that you may have already figured out is to call your phone and listen for the ring tone, but that works only if you serendipitously find yourself near the phone in the first place. That trick works with any phone, but it works *only* with phones, not with tablets.

Get Your Mobile Loaded!

Once you have a mobile device, you will want to add content to it to get the most use and value from it. Content consists of media (e-books, music, pictures, movies) and software that will enhance the device's usability. This is the point where memory becomes an issue and you will likely wish you had more than you got when you bought the device. With Apple devices, you are out of luck because you cannot supplement the memory. With many Android devices, though, you can add memory.

However much memory you have, try to keep at least 10 percent free of content. Doing so helps the device run better and gives the operating system some breathing space. So, if you have a 64 GB device, try to keep at least 6.4 GB available, and if you have a 32 GB device, keep at least 3.2 GB available. Add the software you want and any data that you need to add to use the software; then add media files (movies, music, e-books, audiobooks, and so on), as all work and no play makes Jill dull, dull, dull!

While you are at it, you might want to add some games to the mix. We particularly like those that help seniors keep their mind active. Examples include Scrabble and Four Letters (a game that requires you to form a word with four random letters in the allotted time and gives you a point for each word you form). By the way, the longer you go, the shorter the time gets. Seven Sevens is another good game, offering some basic strategy decisions. Almost any strategy-oriented game that you can play against the device works here. Chess and Backgammon offer other examples. Depending on your personal proclivities, you might also want to add a few arcade games. Nothing like a good shoot 'em up to vent your frustrations! One thing you can count on, both the iTunes App Store and Google's Play Store give you lots of games in many genres to choose among.

You can also add educational courses to your mobile devices and use your spare time to learn a new subject. In addition to Apple's iTunes University, many colleges and universities offer courses online, and you can purchase lectures in audio and video format for a number of college- and high-school-level courses as well as subjects that may interest you, such as photography, cooking, investing, and many others. You might want to check out the offerings at www.thegreatcourses.com. This site sells college-level courses taught by professors from some of the top schools. It usually has some kind of sale going on, so look for discounted pricing before paying the listed price. We have found the offerings interesting and informative and the sale prices reasonable.

We never travel without a good collection of movies, educational programs, reading material, audiobooks, music, and games on our iPads and smartphones.

A Partial List of iOS Apps You May Want

We created the following list just for the Apple aficionados (aka the iOS folks). It is a partial list of software that you may want to have and should probably take a look at while loading your iOS device. We have excluded from this list the apps that come native to the device and the iOS.

Microsoft Word	PowerPoint	Excel
OneNote	Outlook	iBooks
GoodReader	The Weather Channel	Evernote
Scrabble	LoseIt	iBooks
Kindle	Nook	The Fit Brain collection (about ten apps to help train and exercise your brain)
Omni Plan	Omni Focus	Omni Graffle
OmniOutliner	SignMyPad	12E Calculator
World Clock	Alarm Clock	SpeechTimerz
Timer+	Skype	FileMaker Go
Neat	Paperless	Netflix
AOL TV	Flixter	HBO Now

(Continued)

Banking app for each bank with which you do business	Quicken	Binaural health apps (a series of numerous sound effects designed to tune up your brain)
Dropbox	Transporter	One Drive
Hightail	Google+	Duolingo
Translate	Word Lens	Lingvo
iTranslate	CLIO	TabLit
Exhibit A	CaseRoom	Trial Pad
Transcript Pad	LexisAdvance	WestlawNext
Loislaw	CourtDaysPro	Clear+
Remember The Milk	Inspiration	Mindjet Maps
Garage Band	700 City Maps	MapQuest
Ulmon Pro	Waze	Open Table
UrbanSpoon	Zagat	NYT Now
NPR News	CNN	PDF Pen
Sirius XM	Slacker Radio	1Password
LastPass	Timeline	TripIt
FlightBoard	Apps for whatever airlines you normally use	Orbitz
Expedia	Travelocity	Priceline
Triposo	Tripwolf	Fodor's City Guides

(Continued)

Amazon Fire TV	YouTube	Amazon Instant Video
Dictate	Olympus Dictation	Dragon Dictation
Philips Dictation	The Great Courses	Seven Sevens
Four Letters	Reading Assistant	Eye Reader
VPN Unlimited		

A Partial List of Android Apps You May Want

We created the following list just for the Android folks. It is a partial list of software that you may want to get from Google's Play Store.

Google Authenticator	Whatsapp	Spotify
Tune In Radio	PushBullet	Google Play Music
Duolingo	Citymapper	Skyskanner
Photoshop Touch	Google Maps	Waze
You Tube	Play Movies	Play Books
Google Drive	Evernote	Open Table
Scrabble	Nook	Kindle
Google Translate	Netflix	Genius Scan
Move to SDCard	Clean Master	SHO Anytime
OneDrive	Remember the Milk	Dragon Go!
Timers4Me	Audiobooks	Transporter
Great Courses	One Note	Dropbox
TuneInRadio	LastPass	Lumosity

(Continued)

Duolingo	iHeartRadio	Sirius
NYTimes	CityMaps2Go	Phone Tracker
VPN Unlimited	Audio Recorder	Apps for whatever airlines you normally use
Orbitz	Expedia	Travelocity
Priceline	Microsoft Office Mobile	LexisNexis Online
WestlawNext	Banking app for each bank with which you do business	Quicken
CLIO	DocuSign	MapQuest GPS
TripIt	GateGuru	Flightboard
Zagat	Google Drive	LoseIt
WebMD	Four Letters	Adobe Photoshop Express
Triposo World Travel Guide	TripAdvisor	The Great Courses
Ulmon Pro		

Power Makes the World Go Round...

No, we absolutely don't mean the kind of power that corrupts. But, in reality, without power, our mobile devices convert from useful tools to dead weight. Back in the day when mobile phones were the size and weight of a brick, a half hour of talk time maxed out the mobile. We used to carry the phone and several battery packs to allow us to maximize the use of the device. As time went on, battery technology improved, and we got to the point where a mobile device could run for several hours without recharging. We also learned how to build smaller and more powerful batteries to fuel our shrinking devices.

As we started to demand more and more from our mobile devices, the capability of their batteries to continue to power them over prolonged periods of time grew more and more strained. Many heavy users of mobile technology have had to recharge their devices one or more times during a single day to keep the technology running. That works okay if we spend the day next to an electrical outlet but creates issues for us if we do not. Since most of us don't spend the day hanging around electrical outlets, we needed another solution. If your device allows you to open it and replace batteries, that offers you one solution for the problem. If it does not open (you cannot replace batteries in many devices), that solution does not help. But here's one that will: get an external battery and keep it with you to recharge your phone or tablet, as necessary. You can get these batteries in all sorts of configurations and with widely varying capacities to hold power that you can transfer to your mobile devices on the go.

Some of the external batteries come as powered cases for your device (usually a cell phone); others come simply as a power block with ports to accept USB cables. Either way, you charge the battery booster and use that reserve power to charge up your device when its own power supply dwindles. We do not like the powered cases as much as the separate power blocks, so we recommend that you get the blocks. While the powered cases may prove convenient for the device that you put them on, they cannot provide power to other devices. The blocks can power any compatible device. Ideally, you will get one with more than one port so that you can charge two devices at the same time. Some of the devices come with short cables built in, so you do not even have to carry cables with you. MyCharge (www.mycharge.com) makes a series of power boosters with integrated cables for iOS devices (Lightening tips) or other devices (micro USB tips). Some of the MyCharge devices also come with built-in hooks that allow you to clip them to something for easy portability. You can find these devices online (try Amazon.com) and in stores such as Best Buy or Fry's. We have tried a number of them that we like, including (without limitation) MyCharge, Tylt, PowerRocks, Anker, HyperShop, and Mophie (if you want a powered phone case, we like Mophie's the best). We recommend you get one or two power blocks, keep them charged, and carry them with you as insurance against finding yourself powerless. We like the idea of carrying a relatively small one in our pocket at all times and leaving a larger one in a briefcase or purse or even in the car. If you plan to use a tablet on a long plane trip, you will want to bring one along in your carry-on.

Remember that not all devices charge at the same rate. Most of the batteries charge at 1 amp or less. Larger devices, such as tablets, usually require 2.1 amps. They generally can charge off a 1 amp charger, but it will take considerably longer. Many mobile devices can charge off a range of power supplies. Apple's iPhones, for example, will charge off a 1 amp charger, and they even come from Apple with a 1 amp charger. If you connect your iPhone to a 1 amp charger, it will charge just fine. If you connect it to a 2.1 amp charger, it will not explode; it will just charge faster. That works, by the way, for wall plug chargers and battery blocks.

Productivity Apps for Microsoft Office

You can get many apps to make you more efficient and productive; some of them actually work! For our money, however, some of the most important apps to get for your tablet (without regard to whether it works on the Android or the iOS systems) come from Microsoft. Yep, we have Office, right here in our app stores. After holding out for some time, forcing us to use third-party solutions, Microsoft brought the real deal to the table and provided us with the Office Suite for tablets. It then made it available for phones. We recommend you get it right from the start. Microsoft priced the apps right; they cost NOTHING! Not surprisingly, however, Microsoft hid a hook in the bait. You can download the apps and use them to read Office documents, but you cannot use the apps to create or revise those documents **unless** you have a subscription to Microsoft Office 365. They do charge for that.

Microsoft Office 365 comes only on a subscription basis, so you rent the use of the software for a monthly or annual fee. Microsoft offers a number of different plans for personal and business use, including several multiuser plans.

If you use an Android tablet, Microsoft Office is as good as you can get, in our opinion. If you use an Apple tablet, the truth of the matter is that Pages and Keynote are generally superior to Microsoft Word and PowerPoint. While you may want to have Apple's offerings too, we think you should also have Microsoft Word and PowerPoint, as the world has largely standardized on Microsoft Office for the present time.

Can We Talk?

Apple has advertised Siri for some time now. Most of us know that if we have an iOS device, Siri came along for the ride and we can talk to her (it), request information, and have Siri carry out some basic tasks for us. Not to be undone, Google came up with Google Now to do pretty much the same thing, and now Microsoft has brought a date to the party by the name of Cortana. Amazon also has crashed the party with Alexa.

Whether you choose to date Siri, or Cortana or just let Google Now take care of you largely comes down to a matter of personal preference. If you opt for the iPhone, you get Siri; if you go with Android, you get Google Now; and if you choose Windows Phone, Cortana comes along for the ride. You can buy Alexa from Amazon, add her to the mix, and let them fight it out. All have the same basic function: to provide assistance to you and function as a virtual digital assistant to give you reminders, send a text, get some information, or set up a phone call for you.

Can We Talk Some More?

If you send text messages, you can save yourself a lot of hassle by not bothering to type them. If you have an iPhone, you can send a voice message as an SMS or text message. Doing that takes very little effort. You start out as though you were going to send a text message. When you see a little microphone icon at the bottom of the display, simply put your finger on it and press to talk. The microphone icon will expand into a circle with options and record as long as you hold your finger in place. When you are done, press the up arrow and it will send the audio file as though it were a text message You can then see the completed transaction.

Two caveats: (1) the system limits you to approximately ten-second messages; and (2) it works only from iPhone to iPhone. If your recipient has some other brand of phone, you have to go back to plain old texting.

Still Talking!

Telephone and tablet technology have evolved with respect to dictation. Now you can get apps (preferably from the folks at Dragon, now owned by Nuance) that allow you to dictate to your mobile device. Yes, you can actually talk to your device and have it convert your words into text. Please note that we do not recommend that you dictate while driving, even though you can do it with your hands still on the steering wheel. Please wait until you have pulled off the road!

If you have a hard time getting the right keys on a virtual keyboard, you will want these apps and this functionality. Even if you can get the keystrokes right, these apps make it a lot easier to answer your e-mail and do other tasks.

Use Your Tablet to Occupy a Grandchild

Telephone and tablet technology have proven popular with people of all ages. While your grandchildren may not do much damage to the device, you might have to go back and correct some settings if you leave a tablet or a smartphone lying around for them to pick up. If you do not have a good selection of games that they like, they will be more likely to try to find something else entertaining to do with your device. On the other hand, the device can make an excellent ally for a babysitter as young children seem to take to these devices and enjoy playing with them for surprisingly long time periods.

You can get lots of educational games and age-appropriate media for your devices. If you plan on using them this way, you will want to do that. Alternatively, you could just give your grandchild his or her own as a present. Jeff did that for his three year old grandson and five year old granddaughter. The kids use their tablets all the time. Mom and dad control what goes on them (at least for now).

Keep Your Electronics Away from Dogs!

Apparently the human species is not the only one attracted to electronics. When it comes to pets, particularly dogs, you had better consider your tablets and smart-phones as attractive nuisances. We have found that these devices have an almost

irresistible attraction for dogs, and in particular Labrador Retrievers. For some reason, the Labs have gotten it into their heads that these devices are some form of chew toy. Surprisingly, gorilla glass notwithstanding, some dogs (including Labs) have the jaw strength to bite hard enough through a protective case to break the display on an iPad. Buck, the iPad-eating Lab at our house, actually chewed so hard on the iPad inside of the case that he cracked the lower corner of the display. The crack later spidered over the entire display. The moral of that story: keep your devices in protective cases and out of sight and reach of your pets.

Buck, a black Labrador Retriever, has liked Apple products most of his life. He thinks they make great chew toys. So far, he has managed to get his jaws around an iPad and a couple of iPhones. Caveat: we had the Apple extra protection plan and, as a result, Apple replaced the iPad for a nominal ($50) charge. (We managed to save the iPhones which suffered only minor cosmetic damage.)

Tips for Using Your Computer

We chose to separate tips for computers from those for other mobile devices, even though some computers have a high degree of mobility. We did that because the computer really is a completely different animal than a mobile phone, tablet, or phablet. We have seen evidence that the nature of the traditional computer is changing as Apple's operating systems for its computers and mobile devices merge more and more closely. Interestingly, Microsoft tried to jump ahead in the hardware department by merging a tablet and a computer (witness Microsoft's Surface Pro 3 and 4). Apple has moved in the same direction with its iPad Pro. Certainly, the traditional computer has not yet gone the way of the dinosaur, but it appears to have taken the route of the electric typewriter and the magnetic-card-operated word processor. Perhaps many of us did not fully appreciate the significance of Steve Jobs's reference to the "post PC world," but we predict that 10 or 15 years from now, most people will likely not have what today we would call a traditional computer or laptop.

For at least the next five to seven years, however, most of us will continue to use a personal computer, at least in the office, while more and more of us will rely on other devices outside the office. In this section, we focus on buying and using a traditional computer (including both desktop and laptop computers).

While computer software sales have started to move toward the same model as the apps for smartphones and tablets, you can still get lots of software directly from the publisher and easily install it directly on your computer. More and more frequently the vendor will sell the software online and then simply allow you to download it to your computer.

Many vendors have started offering software on a subscription basis, often called software as a service ("SaaS"). This approach has the advantage of giving you updates at no extra cost and with no extra effort. You can use the software through a browser anywhere you have Internet access, but you generally cannot use the software without the Internet (some software, although Internet subscription based, allows you to download a version to your computer and use it off-line). Apple has even added an App Store for computer software to the mix.

In this section, we also identify some of the software that we have found useful for computers, smartphones, and tablets. Many of the programs give you the opportunity to try them out for a period of time or provide a limited-use version for you to try at no cost. We encourage you to take advantage of that opportunity to try the program's features so that you can determine whether it will work well for you.

Microsoft Office 365

Everyone knows or should know about Microsoft Office. It comes in a few different structures that include different programs, four of which serve as the basic core of the suite: Word, PowerPoint, Outlook, and Excel. Most law offices use Microsoft Office or at least a part of it in their practice. Microsoft has created robust Mac iterations of Office with the almost completely perfect capability to move files from the Mac to the Windows to mobile platforms and conversely. (There are still occasional hiccups due to some formatting differences, but the files transfer and can be corrected easily when necessary.)

Microsoft has ventured into the SaaS arena with Microsoft Office and offered Office 365. Office 365 takes advantage of the cloud and comes with a terabyte of storage in the cloud. Not surprisingly, Microsoft offers several different subscription plans designed for business, personal, and educational uses, each of which requires an annual (or, in the case of the educational version, longer) commitment.

The Business Essentials plan costs $5.00 per month per user. It affords an online version of Office with e-mail and video-conferencing. It excludes use on tablets and phones.

The 365 Business version costs $8.25 per user per month and allows use on tablets and smartphones but excludes use of the videoconferencing, e-mail, calendar, and contact features.

The 365 Business Premium version costs $12.50 per user per month and includes all the available features (including tablet and phone use, e-mail, calendar, contacts, and videoconferencing).

If you do not use Outlook as your mail/contacts/calendar program, you should be fine with the Business version. If you do, you will want the Business Premium version. If you have Microsoft Office on your computer already, Microsoft has made it necessary for you to get Office 365 for at least $8.25 per month if you want to use Office directly on your tablet or smartphone. Without Office 365, Office files are available on a read-only basis to your mobile devices through the applicable office program app (alternatively, you can acquire one of the many work-alike apps that let you work with Office files on tablets without actually having Office on your tablet).

Having Office 365 does have some advantages. For example, in some subscription packages, Microsoft lets you install it on up to five devices per subscription. Additionally, you won't have to buy upgrades or new versions of the software; they come as part of the subscription and you can set the software to automatically install the update for you.

For now, Microsoft continues to sell local installations of the Office Suite. It has made purchasing them less favorable, limiting them to a single PC and excluding the ability to use the software with a tablet or phone. We predict that, ultimately, Microsoft will offer Office only through subscription.

Get a Mac

Windows has grown better over time, but we think you have to wonder when a new version of Windows comes out and the pundits describe it as the "most Mac-like yet." Imitation may still prove the sincerest form of flattery; it may also suggest a tacit acknowledgment of superiority. Apple's OS X, the operating system native to the Mac, has a Unix backbone. As a result, it has presented a stable platform for many years and through multiple iterations of the OS. It also has a very user-friendly presentation.

Historically most law offices opted for the Windows OS and, as a result, those writing programs for law offices wrote almost exclusively for the Windows OS, putting Mac users at a theoretical disadvantage. The popularity and widespread adoption of the iPhone and the iPad by attorneys has induced many attorneys to shift to the Mac OS at home and often at work. As more and more attorneys move to the Mac OS, many program developers have shifted their perspective and now produce

Mac and Windows versions of programs. Perhaps more significantly, the evolution of SaaS, offering browser-based access to programs on a platform-agnostic basis, has largely equalized that playing field.

For some time, many have recognized the superiority of Apple's hardware. Once Apple shifted to the use of Intel chips, it became possible to boot a Windows operating system directly on a Macintosh computer. That capability makes the Apple hardware much more flexible than machines built for Windows, because you can run the Mac OS and the Windows OS on an Apple computer, but only the Windows OS on a machine built for Windows. That said, for personal use or in a solo or small firm environment, we think you are better advised getting the Mac (Apple) hardware and running the Mac OS for the following reasons:

- The Mac OS, built on a solid Unix base, has proven more stable than the Windows OS.
- We have found that the Mac OS network is more easily manageable than a Windows OS network.

- You can easily run a Mac OS network without an IT department. It is much more difficult to do so with a Windows network.
- Mac system upgrades tend to cost less than Windows upgrades (most come at no charge).
- Mac OS upgrades tend to install with less hassle and fewer problems than Windows upgrades.
- We think the Mac OS is still more user-friendly than Windows.

Make Your Screen More Readable

As computer displays got better, developers employed higher and higher screen resolutions in building their computers. While higher resolution made the display look smoother and cleaner and present more detail, it also tended to make print look smaller and smaller. As we grow older, many of us will lose the ability to easily read smaller and smaller print. We can wear glasses to help us decipher the smaller print, but the fact remains that, even with glasses, many of us will find some print uncomfortably small to read. If you go to your screen settings, however, you can increase the size of the screen icons as well as the system font, making the display much easier to read. You can do that on both Windows and the Mac OS, although you follow some different steps. You can also easily increase the size of the displayed image/text in many programs.

On the Mac OS, go to System Preferences, select Accessibility, and then choose Display. You will have several options available to you immediately, including making the contrast higher and the cursor size larger. Make whatever adjustments help you read the screen more easily. If you select Open Display Options at the bottom of the window, you can change the display parameters respecting brightness to make the display more easily readable. You can also adjust the resolution by choosing between the default and a scaled option that adjusts the size of everything on the screen without pixelating it.

If you go back to the Accessibility options, you can select Zoom and set up the computer to allow you to zoom in when you need to do so.

If you have Windows 8, the process is a bit different. Go to your desktop and right-click (or go to the search box and search for Display and then select Screen Resolution). Choose Make text and other items larger or smaller, and adjust to meet your own requirements and preferences. You can also choose to change specific parts of the screen, such as title bars, without adjusting the size of the other elements of the display. To do that, go to Settings in the

Display menu. Then go to Change only the text size and pick the item(s) you want to change; then select the size you want. If you want to make the text even easier to read, also choose Bold. Finally, click Apply. You need to log out and back in to see the changes. For more details, go to http://windows.microsoft.com/en-US/windows-8/make-textscreen-larger-smaller/?v = t.

In Windows 10 go to the Start Menu and select Settings. In settings, choose System, then select Display. You will see a slider to change the size of text, apps and other items. Slide it to your left to make it smaller and to your right to make it larger.

Make Documents Look Larger

If you are satisfied with the look of your display images but find that the text looks too small when you work with Microsoft Word, you have a couple of options to make your life easier. One of the options is simply to use a larger font size. While it makes sense to increase the font size at some times, doing so can create other problems, such as changing your pagination, or preventing text from lining up properly on pleading paper. As a practical matter, you will probably want to use either 12- or 14-point type on documents that you file with the court. As older judges may have problems with smaller type and younger judges should not find larger type a problem, we recommend using 14-point type most of the time—the only exception being if you are trying to stay within a page limit. As a practical matter, you may find that 14-point type works better for all your printed matter, since it reads much easier than 12-point type. We recommend that you do not use type fonts smaller than 12 point.

If you still strain to read 14-point type or cannot increase font size to 14, the best way to solve the problem is to adjust the document's display size. Microsoft Word allows you to increase the size of the document display to make the text more readable, without changing the font size. It also allows you to decrease the size to see more of the page or even multiple pages at the same time (note that the functionality of this feature requires having a larger display or more than one monitor to accommodate the display of more than one document). You will find this feature in many programs, not just Microsoft Word.

On PCs, you make documents look larger or smaller quickly by holding down the Control (CTRL) key on your keyboard and moving the scroll wheel forward or backward. Holding CTRL and scrolling forward will enlarge the font, while holding CTRL and scrolling backward will shrink the font. Using this technique, you can adjust the size for your reading comfort without altering the font size.

On the newer Macs, you can achieve the same end by using a reverse pinching motion (start with your thumb and fore-finger touching each other on the trackpad and then slide them away from each other to zoom in (enlarge the image). Reverse the slide (start apart and slide them together to zoom out (reduce the image).

Never Forget to Attach a Document by Using the Codetwo Outlook Attachment Reminder

Ever intend to send an e-mail with an attachment but forget to actually load the attachment? The world of computer users likely consists of two groups: those who have forgotten an attachment and those who will forget an attachment. The bad news is that for those who forgot it, there is nothing we can do for you. What is done is done. The good news is that we have a solution for those of you who have not yet forgotten an attachment. The better news is that those who have made the mistake in the past can use this tool, too!

CodeTwo develops software to benefit Microsoft Outlook and Exchange users. One of the useful tools, the Outlook Attachment Reminder, provides an add-on that prompts you if you click Send on an e-mail and forgot an attachment. The add-on identifies e-mails that are missing attachments by scanning the e-mail for words such as *attached* or *enclosed.* If your e-mail includes one of these words, or a variation, and does not have an attachment, the add-on generates a prompt inquiring whether you forgot an attachment. If yes, you can go back to your e-mail and attach; if no, you can simply select No and the message will continue on its way.

To install the add-on, simply go to www .codetwo.com, download the installer, and launch it on your computer. You should make sure Outlook is closed prior to installing the program. Once you have the program installed on your machine, the add-on is ready to scan your outgoing Outlook e-mail and alert you whenever attachments are missing. Reopen Outlook and you are good to go.

find Your Center with firm Central

Thomson Reuters (TR), a GPSolo Division sponsor, has developed a multiplatform practice-management tool, Firm Central, to help level the playing field for solo and small firm lawyers. If you are a WestlawNext user, your practice will get a boost from Firm Central. The software as a service joins a growing market of cloud-based practice-management tools that promise anytime-anywhere access for lawyers no matter the size of your firm. Because it lives in the cloud, it works on both the Mac OS X and the Windows platforms. You can even access it on your iPad or tablet. This means every client document, case law, and time and expense entry is captured and available in one easily retrievable place.

Firm Central was designed to be exactly what it is called—the hub, or center, of your firm. You not only can handle the business of practicing law here but also can conduct your research, gather knowledge, and better manage it to share with your team members. The addition of time and billing to the powerhouse software completes the picture.

A Glance at the Firm Central Dashboard

Firm Central integrates well with several useful tools that support your practice. They include

- Matter and Document Organization
- Unique Integration
- Global Search
- Time and Billing Management
- Client Portal
- Calendar
- Deadline Assistant
- Enhanced Mobility

The Client Portal is a nice addition to the software since it was originally rolled out. With this feature, you can invite clients to collaborate and share information in a secure environment. The portal allows you to share messages, documents, forms, and other case details with your clients.

We recommend that if you are going to use a public cloud, you use it to run applications and store nonprivileged data or nonprotected health information if applicable. Use a semiprivate cloud that you have properly vetted from a well-established and reliable provider familiar with the needs of law firms, such as Thomson Reuters, and/or a properly protected private cloud for files with your personal, privileged, or protected information. By way of example, Thomson Reuters Firm Central employs several layers of security to protect your data, including

- AES 256-bit encryption to encrypt the data stored on your servers
- 2048-bit SSL certificates for data in transit
- Secured data centers with physical and geographic redundancy
- Nightly backups of data stored on its servers
- Highly restricted internal employee access to customer-stored data
- A viable procedure for switching from one server to another in the event of a problem with the primary server

We have toured West's data storage facility utilized for its Firm Central operation and took due notice of the restrictive access and impressive backup measures employed by West at that facility.

Try Doodle to Organize Your Events and Conference Calls

Doodle (www.doodle.com) has created an online scheduling tool that makes scheduling meetings with multiple parties easier. You can poll potential attendees with a selection of dates and times to identify when maximum attendance will be possible. The tool walks you through the process in four simple steps:

1. Create an event.
2. Propose a range of times and dates.
3. Choose your poll settings.
4. Invite participants to your poll.

Creating an event is simple: fill out the Doodle form with the title, location, and description of the event. This information will be conveyed to your poll participants. Enter your name as administrator, along with your e-mail address, to receive a link to view, update, or edit the poll.

In the next step, you can select several date and time ranges. These can even be nonconsecutive dates and times. If you are scheduling a web or teleconference, and your potential attendees are in multiple time zones, we recommend that you enable Time-Zone Support to avoid time zone conversion confusion. Time-Zone Support presents the options to participants in their own time zone, saving the participants the need to convert and the potential confusion and/or embarrassment of making the wrong adjustment to the time.

You can adjust your poll settings to suit your needs. For example, you can make this a Yes/No poll ("Yes, I can make this time" or "No, that time is not good for me") or make it a Yes/No/If need be poll, in which users can identify times that they are available but do not prefer. You also can hide the poll from other participants to keep each potential attendee's schedule and availability confidential from the other poll participants. If you are interested in controlling the size of each meeting, you can limit the number of participants per option. Using this feature will remove an option once the designated number of participants has selected it.

You can invite participants to your poll via e-mail, Facebook, or Twitter. You can link your e-mail account with your Doodle account to import addresses for participants you intend to invite.

The basic scheduling Doodle service is free, with unlimited polls and participants available. You can add features such as ad-free experience or SSL encryption by upgrading to Doodle Premium, but we find this to be an unnecessary expense.

You can use this tool for professional meetings or personal social events with friends and family. It sure beats calling everyone and trying to coordinate that way.

Manage Your Practice and Billing Anywhere with CLIO

"Money makes the world go round."

If you enjoy Broadway musicals, we chose to start this practical tip with a line from a song from the musical *Cabaret*. If you are not into musicals, the point still stands. A law office survives because it bills time and recovers payment for the efforts expended on behalf of clients. Lawyers who do not keep regular time records generally lose a considerable amount of their billings. Lawyers who bill on an hourly basis need to recognize a basic rule of law office business: "Clients almost never pay for time unless you bill them for it."

One of the most essential pieces of law office software, then, is a time and billing program. To function well, it has to work, it has to be easy to use, and it has to be easy to access. We particularly like CLIO:

- It works on multiple platforms.
- As it is cloud-based, you can access it anywhere and from any device with an Internet connection.

- It is easy to use.
- It handles both your operating and your trust accounts interactively and smoothly.
- It simply works!

Note that CLIO has other features available, including contacts management, calendaring, and documents management. These features function competently, but other solutions do them as well or better, in our opinion. We don't care: CLIO's claim to fame and to your computer real estate is billing. For a small firm or solo practice, we have not found anything we like better. If you use a Mac, we have found nothing we like as much.

Using CLIO, you can record time, expenses, and payments or generate bills from anyplace in the world and send them by e-mail to clients or to your office, where your staff can print and snail-mail or e-mail them. CLIO provides its services on a subscription basis, starting at $39 per user per month (based on annual billing). For more details, see www.goclio.com. Clio also offers an app that works on your smartphone or tablet. We prefer the web version, even on the tablet, but the app works better on smartphones due to the relatively diminutive screen size of the phones (even the larger ones).

Turn Outlook into a Practice Management Tool with Credenza

If you use Microsoft Outlook and want to turn your Outlook into practice management software, check out the Microsoft Outlook add-on Credenza from Gavel and Gown, Inc., the company behind Amicus Attorney. Credenza provides an innovative practice management solution that runs as part of Microsoft Outlook. It is a handy solution for lawyers, accountants, consultants, or other professionals who want to organize their information around client files, matters, or projects. Microsoft Outlook alone cannot do this. You can use Categories and tasks to some extent, but when it comes to organizing around matters and clients, Outlook falls short.

With Credenza, you can organize e-mails, appointments, tasks, documents, notes, research, and phone calls. Installation and setup are quick and easy, and the software has a highly customizable interface. You can organize a new project as a Matter, File, Case, Project, or any other name you can come up with. You can set a default type of project or matter and add your own categories if you do not find them already listed in the program.

Credenza offers two versions: Basic and Pro. Credenza Basic comes as a free Microsoft add-on. Basic allows one user to use the e-mail management, Calendaring, Task Management, Contacts, Notes, Files, Time Sheets, and Document Management features. Credenza Pro, which costs $24.95 per month per user, has all the basic features; plus, you can share these features with members of your team. With Pro, you can also take calls and messages for other users in your team and have access to cloud-based document management. Pro also allows you to use invoice and billing features.

Credenza supports Outlook 2003, Outlook 2007, Outlook 2010 (32-bit), and Outlook 2013 (32-bit) on Windows XP, Windows Vista, Windows 7, and Windows 8. Although the website (www.credenzasoft. com) does not list the software as supporting Windows 10, it does appear to work with Windows 10. Since Credenza is an

Outlook add-on, it will run on Mac computers if you set up a Windows environment with Outlook installed using Parallels or some other Windows system emulator. To protect your Outlook data, Credenza sets up a separate database for its use. Using Credenza will not corrupt your Outlook data storage; the add-on uses a separate database to keep its data separate.

Outfox Your Friends on the Computer with Lynda.com

Lynda.com offers a wealth of learning tools focusing on technology. It is an online learning company with the goal of helping anyone learn business, software, technology, and creative skills to achieve personal and professional goals. With a lynda.com subscription, members receive unlimited access to a vast library of high-quality, current, and engaging video tutorials taught by recognized industry experts. The website will help you brush up on your business skills, or you can get training to take your photography or video hobbies to the next level. Membership plans currently break out as follows:

Plan:	Basic Month-to-month	Basic Annual Billing	Premium Month-to-month	Premium Annual Billing
Cost:	$24.99 per month	$19.99 per month	$34.99 per month	$29.99 per month

(Continued)

Benefits:	Access to 3,541 courses	Access to 3,541 courses	Access to 3,541 courses	Access to 3,541 courses
			Access downloadable exercise files to work along with the instructors	Access downloadable exercise files to work along with the instructors
				View files offline with your iOS or Android device

You can start with a free trial to see if you find the lessons helpful before the website starts charging you. As with most free trials, you have to set up an account and payment method. You must notify the site you wish to cancel before it charges you. The free trial lasts ten days. You can sign up for any of the plans during your free trial and downgrade to a less-expensive plan to avoid the extra cost. This is a good way to see if the premium services are worth the extra charge.

Google Search Tips

The Google search engine is a powerful tool for a variety of tasks and problems. It is widely used today for almost every searching need. How many times have you heard someone say, "Just Google it"?

Use the Tabs

On the top of every Google search page, you see the Web, Image, News, and More tabs. Choosing one of these tabs can hone your search results to what you are looking for. If you are looking for a news article, select News. You can then further limit the range of search to a specific date range.

Use Quotation Marks [""] to Find an Exact Phrase

Using quotation marks allows you to specify the sequence that words appear in— for example, "ab initio"—and prevents you from getting results that focus on *ab* or *initio* alone. Unless you are in the market for an ab machine, feel free to leave the quotes off so that you can multitask while you search.

Search by File Type

Search for a specific type of file, such as PDF, PPT, or XLS, by adding the file type and the three-letter file abbreviation.

Quickly Find the Time

In the search bar, you can type "Time Houston" or anywhere in the world you would like to know the time, and Google will instantly pull it up, along with what time zone the location is in.

Track Your Packages

Track your UPS, FedEx, or USPS packages by typing the tracking number directly into the search box. The results will show you the status of your shipment.

Tips for Using the Internet to Communicate with Friends and Family

One of the many things that the Internet enables us to do is communicate extensively and easily with family and friends both geographically nearby and in disparate locations. No parent or grandparent should lack the knowledge of how to talk to his or her children and grandchildren using Voice Over Internet Protocol (VOIP) software, instant messaging, chat, and videoconferencing. Not that long ago my (Jeff's) adult daughter chided me for giving my original iPhone to my wife instead of her when I upgraded to a newer model. Her stinging accusation: "Mom [who was then already a senior] doesn't even know how to text message!" Needless to say, Mom [now a few years older] has learned to text message and does so regularly with all the family members except for grandchildren still too young to have cell phones (although she still prefers to talk to them on the phone).

In this section, we explore some of the ways you can communicate with business associates, friends, and family using the Internet and various computer and mobile device software.

Cut the Wires!

Do you still rely on a hard-wired telephone system?

Would you like to have the ability to call all over the world without significant telephone charges?

Would you like the ability to have videoconferences with friends and family without significant equipment and usage charges?

If you answered any of those questions affirmatively, consider switching from hard-wired telephone systems (including those that wire to a base station and then support wireless extensions) to a VOIP system. VOIP (Voice Over Internet Protocol) uses the Internet to transmit information. VOIP systems can use standard wired telephones or softphones (software phones using the computer) to communicate. The softphone provides a significant advantage in that it makes it easy to use video-calling capabilities without buying expensive videoconferencing equipment. You can get simple plug-and-play VOIP systems to use at home or far more sophisticated systems capable of running your office. The best news: VOIP systems generally cost significantly less to set up and operate than a hard-wired system.

facebook

Since its launch in 2004, Facebook has become one of the most popular social networking sites on the Internet. While the bulk of its users are not yet 40, it has proven to be an excellent way for all family members to keep in touch. One of my (Ashley's) parents used Facebook to find relatives across the country and assembled a 50th wedding anniversary for my grandparents. Facebook opened a door to a whole other world of family that I would never have met had this medium not existed.

In fact, my parents and grandparents use Facebook more than I do, partly due to their retirement and mild addiction to the games offered. The real draw to social media for seniors is the convenience, accessibility, and low expense of online interaction with loved ones located anywhere in the world. Getting started is easy. To begin, go to www.facebook.com. After you enter your basic information, the site walks you through setting up a profile. You can add a picture to make your profile more personal or skip that step and leave the profile picture blank. After you finish this step, the registration requires you to check the e-mail you provided and confirm your registration. You will see an e-mail from Facebook security.

At this point, you should write down the confirmation code and then click the blue bar that reads "Confirm Your Account" to complete your confirmation process. Clicking the bar will take you back to Facebook, where any of the contacts you had with the e-mail account you used will be listed as "People You May Know." You may even have a few contacts that already sent you connection requests. With permission, Facebook will send a request to anyone on your e-mail contact list, so if your e-mail was on someone else's contact list and that person agreed, Facebook would have sent you a connection request already.

At this stage, you are well on your way to making connections and staying in touch with multiple generations of family and friends, all from your computer. If you use a smartphone, you can download the app and carry this communication portal wherever you go.

facetime

If you own an Apple iPad or iPhone, Face-Time comes with the device as part of the iOS. FaceTime, Apple's video chat program, allows you to see and hear the person you call. It requires an Internet connection and the person on the other end must use FaceTime as well. If you have someone you haven't seen in a while, and both of you have Apple devices, FaceTime gives you a wonderful way to communicate with him or her.

With a good connection, this program works well. If both you and the person you are contacting are on Wi-Fi and have iOS 7 or higher, you can also use FaceTime as a VOIP solution, making phone calls that do not use up your minutes.

Under Settings, you will find a menu devoted to your FaceTime Settings. This menu gives you the option of toggling the feature on or off. It shows your Apple ID and allows you to list contacts through which people can reach you using Face-Time. It also lets you toggle whether to allow FaceTime to run over cellular or to limit its use to Wi-Fi. Choosing to allow FaceTime to run over cellular makes it available to use anywhere you have a cell phone signal, but this can be an expensive choice. If you have a limited data package, you will quickly eat through your data allowance.

To start using FaceTime, from the home screen of your smartphone or iPad, tap the FaceTime app icon. This green icon has a white video camera inside. Once you open the app, you will notice a search bar at the top of the screen. Tapping inside the search bar allows you to enter the name or phone number of the person you wish to FaceTime with. Alternatively, you can tap the + symbol in the top-right corner of the screen. This pulls up your device's contact list, and you can scroll to the person you wish to contact and select him or her. When you tap the contact, the contact's information is displayed, and then you can tap the FaceTime button (which looks like a little video camera) next to the contact's stored phone number or e-mail address. Be sure to double-check that you are using the appropriate method for placing a Face-Time call: if you're calling an iPhone user, you should use a phone number; if you're calling an iPad, iPod touch, or FaceTime for Mac user, you need to make the call using that person's e-mail address.

You can also call someone via FaceTime from within the person's Contact profile. To do this, either go directly to your Contacts app, or tap the green-and-white phone icon for your phone app, and then tap contacts; it is the middle icon at the bottom of your screen, a circle with a shaded silhouette inside.

Some pointers may prove helpful:

- FaceTime works better when both parties have a reliable wireless connection. For short FaceTime video chats, 3G (third-generation cellular technology generally referred to as "3G" by providers) will suffice, but the application may demand too much data to maintain a reliable 3G connection.
- If you want to sit and video chat with someone, it's helpful to stand your iPhone up against something such as a shelf so that you don't have to keep holding your phone an arm's length away from your face.

Twitter

Twitter is an information network made up of 140 character messages called tweets. Twitter offers an easy way to discover the latest news related to subjects you care about. Think of it as a thought-sharing platform where the only filters are you ... and the character limitation. People can post and share their thoughts at any time on any given day. This makes Twitter an excellent platform for establishing, or broadcasting, your brand.

To start using it, go to https://twitter.com. On the screen, you will see a box with bold print that reads "New to Twitter?" Start there. Once you have entered your full name, e-mail address, and a password, click the Sign up for Twitter button. Clicking this button takes you to a page that reads "Join Twitter today," with the first three fields already completed with the information you entered on the previous page.

The next empty field asks for a username. If this Twitter account is for your professional practice, choose your username accordingly (we recommend you avoid "Rock Dude" unless your practice actually involves geology or rock music). The username will be part of your brand and can be as simple as the name of your practice or more complicated as necessary. Keep in mind that you want your target audience to find you. Don't feel too pressured here, though; you can change your username anytime without affecting your Twitter account by editing your profile information.

If you find yourself completely drawing a blank, have no fear; Twitter will offer some suggestions based on your name. Once you settle on a username, simply click the Sign Up button and *voila*! You are on your way.

From here, you can tailor your Twitter experience to meet your needs. Twitter will ask what topics interest you. Topics include Popular Accounts (web celebrities, some real ones), Music, Sports, Photography, Entertainment, Funny, News, Technology (we urge you to consider selecting this one), Fashion, Television, Health, and Gaming. After you choose a few, Twitter will recommend accounts you may be interested in following. You can pick and choose from those selections or choose to follow all the suggestions (just to get your Twitter feed rolling).

When you move past this page, you reach an important stage: your Twitter profile. If your goal is to develop and nurture your online presence, spend some time here. You will see a blank profile with only your username preceded by the @ sign; all Twitter accounts use it. Here, you have the opportunity to add a picture to your profile; we suggest you do so. You want to make a connection with your target audience; you need to give them a face or an image of some sort to connect with.

Continuing on, you have an opportunity to allow Twitter to use your e-mail accounts to find the Twitter accounts of people you may know, or at least people you have exchanged e-mails with in the past. You may want to skip this step until you have finished creating your profile and maybe posted a few tweets.

The next stage presents you with your official Twitter page. At this point, we recommend you go to the gray icon with a white oval inside, located at the top-right corner of the screen. Clicking this icon pulls up a menu showing the View Profile option. Click that link now. Here, you can see the profile that the rest of the world will see if they look for you. Clicking the Edit Profile link pulls up some fields on the left side of the screen where you can add a bio, location, and your website. If you have the information for all three, you should fill out all three fields. You can decide whether to add a location, but you definitely need to include the other two if you want to advertise your practice or establish your brand. Once this step is complete, you are ready to begin tweeting.

A Note about the @ Sign and Twitter

The @ sign is an important code used to refer to individuals on Twitter. It is combined with a username and inserted into tweets to refer to that person or send him or her a public message (for example: @ username). When @ precedes a username, it automatically gets linked to that user's profile page.

Tweet Tips

Tweets are 140-character messages that you post to Twitter. The subject of these messages can be anything you want them to be. You can use tweets for personal social networking or to grow your professional brand, or both. However, if you would like to do both, we recommend you use a separate account for each purpose. If you do set up two accounts, you need to carefully guard against using your professional account for personal tweets.

If you use Twitter to market your practice or to develop your brand, your tweets should focus on demonstrating knowledge and experience in your area of expertise. You can accomplish this by using the following techniques:

- Share links to informative articles that center on your area of authority (better yet, articles you have written on the subject). Give a snippet of your opinion on the matter or an observation of interesting insights to personalize it.

- Consider repeating your tweet multiple times, spacing out the retweet by six to eight hours. People check their tweet feeds sporadically, so you can hit more of your target audience if you retweet throughout the day. Be careful not to retweet too often, however, or your message may start to look like spam. There are websites and apps that can help you schedule the tweets to post, so you do not have to return to Twitter on a schedule. If you want more information about this, check out https://buffer. com.
- If you attend a conference, use the conference hashtag in your tweet. A hashtag is the # symbol, known to many as the pound sign, placed in front of a word, which then causes this word to become a link that anyone can click on or search to find all tweets with that same hashtag. Using this approach also makes it easier to find others with similar interests who may be attending the same conference or to show your diligent

study of the latest developments in the area covered by the conference.

When you start on Twitter, you might want to spend some time promoting others before you jump in to self-promotion. This advice seems counterintuitive since you joined Twitter to showcase your expertise, but think of it as showing that you have good taste and can recognize talent. This approach will help you get to know others in the Twitter community and can prompt others to want to help promote your news when the time comes. As an aside, some of the people you promote may choose to follow you and that may induce others to follow you as well. Following you means that people get your tweets, so having a lot of followers generally means a wider circulation of your posts.

Pinterest

Pinterest (www.pinterest.com) functions as a giant, collaborative pin board. It works as a social bookmarking site, similar to Digg or StumbleUpon. After registering, users can upload, save, and sort images (referred to as "pins") through collections called "pinboards." You can create a pinboard for any category that comes to mind (home improvement, books to read, places to visit, recipes, fitness tips, and so on). Images are required for anything you post. You can create group pinboards with friends and family members to share ideas and collaborate on joint projects or interests.

For your convenience, we offer some Pinterest terminology:

Pin	(v) Share a bookmark on Pinterest, or (n) a bookmark that you share.
Repin	(v) Share someone else's pin on Pinterest.
Board	(n) A categorical association where you organize the posts you have pinned or repinned.

You can share interesting websites to bookmark them for later, as long as you have an image you can use for the pin. You can download a "Pin It" button for your web browser, which makes it easier to pin interesting websites to your boards. You can pin articles (maybe about your firm or on a topic of interest relevant to your firm or your practice areas). You also can pin your firm's website or links to things of personal interest, such as recipes.

Getting started is relatively easy. You can sign up by creating a profile with an e-mail address and password, or you can set it up to connect to your Facebook account. During the initial sign-up, you can pick out categories of interest so that Pinterest can recommend potential pins for you.

You can use Pinterest as part of your social media marketing for your law practice. If you like, you can join Pinterest as a business. You can also convert your personal account to a business account at any time. Since Pinterest is a giant pinboard for people looking for things to plan, buy, or do, you can market the planning side of your services (estate planning, for example, or business planning perhaps). For an example, look at how WikiHow uses Pinterest to post how-tos. You could use your business Pinterest account to post client newsletter articles, how-tos, or checklists that direct users to your website.

Tumblr

Tumblr (www.tumblr.com) is a microblogging platform and social networking website. The website allows you to post multimedia and other content to a short-form blog, which makes posting much easier (you will not feel overwhelmed with the need to fill up space with your words). It is a good way to test the waters of the blogging world before you go all-in with a professionally developed blog. Users can follow other users' blogs, as well as make their blogs private. If you are just starting out with blogging, you may want to make your blog private until you get in a few posts and shake off any rookie mistakes. Tumblr makes it easy to share anything and everything. You can post text, photos, quotes, links, music, and videos from anywhere, including your web browser, phone, or desktop.

This website hosts millions of blogs with billions of posts, so you will not be alone in this microblogging world. It is rapidly gaining popularity, even more so than Facebook for the under-25 generation.

Ready to Move on from Microblogging?

If you have tried your hand at microblogging and want to establish a full-blown blog, here are some tips to get you started. Blogging can be a great tool for promoting your law practice or your hobbies or services. With a well thought out blog, you can maintain a strong online presence and leave potential clients with a positive impression of your competency—not to mention the benefit an informative blog can provide the community. In my (Jeff's) youth, a teacher once told me that every time an elder passes, it is as if a library has burned down. You can influence the next generation by sharing your knowledge on the web.

Many lawyers who publish blogs are becoming known as experts in the area they market themselves. Blogging has proven one of the most effective ways to develop your niche. Here are some of the top reasons to start a blog:

- **Gain Exposure.** A well-maintained blog can expand your web presence and establish you as an expert.

- **Develop a Brand.** Your professional brand highlights the unique value that sets you apart from other attorneys within your niche.
- **Attract New Clients.** The days of pulling out the yellow pages and flipping to the "Lawyers" section are almost gone. Today, clients seeking legal help tend to turn to search engines like Google. A blog is a great way to gain the attention of prospective clients and convince them that you are the person to hire.

- **Generate New Opportunities.** The more you develop your blog, the more people will learn about you and your organization. A thoughtful blog can open doors to new opportunities such as speaking engagements, job leads, invitations to conferences, writing opportunities with other publications, guest blogging gigs, book deals, and a host of other opportunities that might not have found you if you did not blog.

Starting a blog takes time and thoughtful planning. Following are some points to consider before you start:

- **Identify your intended audience.** You can use this marketing tool to target current clients, prospective clients, lawyers in your practice area, the general lawyer population, or the public at large. You may want to target more than one potential audience. In that case, you can aim for content that applies to all or rotate your comments, highlighting new developments of interest to each potential audience.
- **Start off with a private trial run to ensure you have the time to devote the attention your blog needs.** Several sites enable you to set up a blog quickly and start posting content before the site goes live (check out Tumblr for a quick practice run). Try it out for a little while and see if you can afford the time commitment. If you can handle it, take the blog live.

If the time commitment is too great, or if you don't particularly like to write, then blogging may not be the best route for you. Fear not; several other social media marketing tools can still work effectively with fewer time demands.

Build a Better Blog with Graphics

Blog posts can be useful and informative tools, but blog posts with graphics are better. Simply put, posts with graphics tend to be easier to read, ultimately leading to more shares, giving you more bang for your marketing bucks. Graphics are useful for illustrating important points to your readers and breaking up text to make content easier to read; plus, they can make social shares of your post stand out in a news feed.

There is no need to panic. With a few tips, you can be well on your way to creating unique graphics to pair with your blog for that added oomph.

- **Find good photos.** You can use photos you have taken, or tons of sources for photos are out there, some are free, and some require a small fee for use. Some require that you attribute the original author, so make sure you check the requirements before you use an image.

You might want to start with these sources:

- www.freeimages.com
- https://unsplash.com
- www.flickr.com/creativecommons
- **Use Effective Screenshots.** If the content you are posting includes tutorial or how-to information, you can get a lot from a screenshot. You can take screenshots from within Microsoft Word or OneNote. Free tools like Jing allow you to not only capture screenshots but also easily annotate them.
- **Ready to try a little graphics design? Check out Canva.** Canva (www.canva.com) is free design software. Some of the graphics or images you use can cost around $1. With Canva, you can adjust the graphics with text, backgrounds, and custom layouts to enhance your blog content. Signing up and getting started are fast and easy. Canva begins with a 25-second tutorial that gives you all the information you need to know to be on your way. You can also upload

your own photos and use the Canva design tools. With this website and a few choice images from freeimages.com or unsplash.com, you have all the tools you need to create some great, unique graphics for your blog posts.

LinkedIn

LinkedIn (www.linkedin.com) is a business-oriented social media service. Its main purpose is professional networking with the idea that you can find a job, potential clients, sales leads, or potential partners through a database of shared professional connections.

To start using LinkedIn, you need to register and create a LinkedIn "profile." During registration, you will provide some basic personal information: name, e-mail address, location, current employer, and where you went to college. You will have the opportunity to fill out more detailed information on your profile page.

Your LinkedIn profile should read like a resume, with your career, experience, and education highlighted, rather than hobbies or interests. To fill out your profile page, you begin by creating separate entries for each of your current and former jobs—job title, employer, industry, dates, and a short description of what the job entailed. A successful profile should convey to prospective clients that you are at the top of the practice area. Completing the profile involves a lot of steps, and you can get started with an incomplete profile, but you should really take the time to fill out all of the content areas. LinkedIn ranks complete profiles higher in the search results.

You can assess the completeness of your profile by the strength meter located on the right side of the screen as you are going through the setup process. The stronger your profile is, the more complete it appears to be to LinkedIn, and the higher it will rank in search results. When your profile is complete, you will achieve "all-star" profile status. Following are some tips to make sure your profile is all it can be:

- Use an updated professional photo, either of yourself or one that represents your business.
- Highlight the background and work experience relevant to the clients or work opportunities that you want to attract.
- Connect with your current and past clients; they are excellent sources of referrals and that is what LinkedIn was designed to facilitate.

- Share a status update every day. It can be a comment on a change in the law, a link to an interesting article on the subject matter you practice in, or recognition of a colleague's success. It is fairly easy to find something interesting to comment on once a day.

After you add your work and education experience, LinkedIn will suggest members who went to the same school or worked at the same company, helping you expand your network to your fellow alumni. You also can add a summary to your profile, a great place to highlight your professional experience and skills.

Beware of LinkedIn Endorsements and Recommendations

If you actively use LinkedIn, you may have seen an e-mail at some point informing you that a contact has endorsed you for a certain skill. An endorsement may seem innocent enough, but attorneys should be mindful of how their state views LinkedIn endorsements, in order to avoid a potential ethical rules violation. For instance, under ABA Model Rule 7.1, a lawyer may not make any false or misleading claims about his or her services. It appears that if a lawyer permits an endorsement to remain on his or her LinkedIn profile that he or she knows to be misleading, even if someone else posted the endorsement, it could pose a problem under Rule 7.1.

Also consider, if you, the lawyer, respond to receiving an endorsement by giving your contact a similar endorsement for his or her service, you may be coming up on a violation of Model Rule 7.2(b), which limits a lawyer's ability to give anything of value to a person for recommending the lawyer's services, except under the outlined exceptions.

Handling endorsements is a gray area, but worth treading over carefully.

Tips for Sharing Media

As we have grandchildren and start to dote on them, it becomes more and more important that we get updated pictures of them. Accordingly, seniors want and need to know how to share media with their children (the doting parents who take many of those pictures). As grandparents will want to take many of their own pictures, the sharing becomes a two-way street, since the doting parents will likely want copies of the pictures that grandma and grandpa take. Technology and the Internet provide many options for sharing pictures among a group of people. We explore some of those options with you in this section.

The term *media* includes a great deal more than pictures. It also includes home videos, movies, television shows, educational courses, music, printed and audio books, podcasts, electronic document files, and more. For a variety of reasons, we want to share media with others on a personal and a professional level. This section offers some help, guidance, and tips on how to do that safely and securely.

Dropbox

Dropbox (www.dropbox.com) is a free web-based file-sharing service that lets you bring your photos, documents, and videos anywhere and share them easily with others. The service enables you to drop any file into a designated folder on your computer or laptop. Dropbox then synchs that folder with Dropbox's Internet service and any of your other computers and devices linked to the same account that have an operating Internet connection with the Dropbox client. You can also upload files manually through a web browser. By installing Dropbox on multiple computers and linking those computers to the same account, you can keep the information in that folder synchronized to all of those computers. The process occurs automatically, as long as you leave the computers turned on and connected to the Internet. If you turn off a computer or it has no Internet connection, it can automatically start the update process as soon as you turn it back on and connectivity is restored.

You can even add Dropbox to tablets and smartphones and access the information in the Dropbox folder from those devices.

Dropbox also enables you to share folders inside your Dropbox folder with others who do not have general access to your Dropbox folder or to other content in that folder.

In the past, Dropbox had some security issues. These problems seem to have been solved, but as a precaution, we recommend that you encrypt important and confidential data before storing it in Dropbox.

Dropbox offers a basic account with relatively limited storage free to everyone. Should you need more storage for your data, you can rent it for a fee.

Family Sharing with iCloud

Apple's Family Sharing with iCloud makes it possible for up to six people in your family to share photos, a family calendar, and more to help keep everyone connected. Either you or another adult in your life can start it. The person who starts the sharing is the "organizer." If you're the organizer, you can go into the Settings of your iPhone or iPad and tap iCloud. From there, when you see a link to Family, tap that bar to open it. Here, you can invite up to five additional family members, but you (or the organizer) have to agree to pay for any iTunes, iBooks, and App Store purchases that your family members initiate while part of the family group. Once family members join, iCloud installs features of Family Sharing on all family members' devices. This tool may work for better for sharing with your significant others more so than your grandchildren or younger generations, depending on how prone they are to purchasing and downloading music, books, and apps.

When Family Sharing is turned on, a shared album is set up automatically in the Photos app on all family members' devices. Then everyone can add photos, videos, and comments to the album and be notified when something new is added. Family Sharing also creates a family calendar where everyone can view, add, or change events and appointments. Members of your Family group can also get an alert when something changes. Anyone can use the Reminders app to send time or location reminders to the family as well. So, for example, when it's your anniversary or any important occasion, or even the start of a family vacation, everyone's in the know.

Cozi

Cozi (https://my.cozi.com/signup) is a free shared calendar app available on iPhone, iPad, iPod touch, and Android devices. You can keep track of your family's plans and even send to-do lists to each other, making it perfect for coordinating schedules and calendars, and for keeping your work and home life in balance. You can invite people to share your calendar from within the app, or you can set up everything in your web browser. Once you have created a free account, you can add calendar items, get e-mail reminders and send them to everyone sharing the calendar, keep a shared shopping or to-do list, and even maintain a family journal where you can share photos and stories and jot down fun moments for everyone to see. You can set the Cozi web application as your home page, making it faster to access everything when you sit down at the computer.

Trello

A free collaborative task manager app, Trello (www.trello.com) can come in handy in helping you manage tasks or matters with a partner or staff member. The app allows you to drag and drop task cards and lists, personalize cover images, add check-lists, and create new boards. To collaborate with others, just have them install Trello on their devices and set up an account. You can add users by name, and any changes you make will be synced in real time. Once all your users are added to the project, you will have a visual overview of what everyone is working on and who is working on what project.

Trello works as a project management system made up of boards, lists, and cards. Project (or matter) managers can create a board for each matter that a team is handling. You might want a list for tasks with questions or needing clarification, so your team members can move cards over there for your review when you are not at the office. You can add cards under each list for the tasks or action items and assign a team member to each card. Each team member can make notes on the progress, add questions, or mark it as finished when complete. At the start of filing, you can create a "Deadlines" board and list the upcoming deadlines for everyone to be aware of. Trello basically acts as a white board that lets you organize and create lists that work with how you think.

Oh, and did we mention that it does not cost you anything? Go to the website, set up your account, and start organizing!

Instagram

Instagram is an online mobile photo-sharing, video-sharing, and social networking service that allows you to take pictures or videos and share them on a variety of social networking platforms, including Facebook and Twitter. You use Twitter to communicate in short sentences; you use Instagram to communicate through visual images.

The Instagram app is available free through Apple's iTunes App Store and Google's Play Store. It allows you to share photos or videos with friends and family who follow you. Similar to Facebook contacts, when you set up an Instagram account, Instagram can connect you with friends and family based on your contact list, and you can follow them, if you want. They will also receive notification and can follow you. If they follow you, they will see the photos or videos you take and post through the app. You can "like" photos and comment on them similar to the way you would treat posts on Facebook.

When you take a picture with the app or upload a photo from your phone's camera roll to share, you can edit the image and apply filters to lend cool effects to the photos. You can also scale and crop the images to show what you want to show.

Instagram uses hashtags (for example, #cooltechtip), so you can tag photos with a similar thread. Tagging helps categorize or organize your images. If you take a picture of the Grand Canyon and share it with the hashtag #grandcanyon, you may find a host of similar photos taken by other users. This is an interesting way to feel connected.

Photobucket

Photobucket offers a free image-hosting website with nearly 10 billion hosted photos already, making it a popular way to share and edit photos. It offers unlimited photo and video storage (although it has limits on file size), album organization, Facebook integration, and mobile apps. You can even edit photos from your mobile device by downloading a partner app called Snapbucket. It offers 10 GB of monthly bandwidth and a 5 MB limit for photos on the free account (paid subscribers can get up to 20 MB per photo). Photobucket gives you a lot of ways to share your photos with friends and social networks. It also provides photo-editing tools.

Everyone has heard of spring cleaning as the practice of thoroughly cleaning the home in the springtime. But you shouldn't think of spring cleaning solely in terms of cleaning your *physical space*; it is also a great time to clean your digital space. With Photobucket, you can edit, delete, move, and organize several photos at once on your desktop or mobile device. These bulk actions can save you time and make it easy to keep your photos organized. Once you have your photos loaded, you can create albums and subalbums with the click of a button to help easily find the photos you are looking for when you are looking for them. You can organize albums by birthdays, vacations, anniversaries ... or any category or event you choose.

Picasa and Picasa Web Album

Picasa is an excellent choice for a handy and free photo-management program that you download from http://picasa.google. com. Once you have it downloaded, you can do the following:

- Transfer photos from camera to computer
- Delete the photos you don't want to keep, and rename or add captions to the keepers
- Organize the photos with folders, albums, tags, faces, and places
- Find and view photos on your computer
- Edit pictures; make them look better with easy single-click features that rival much more complex photo-editing software
- Prepare and resize pictures for use in other programs
- Share via print, e-mail, and websites
- Back them up!

In addition to the desktop software, you have access to Picasa Web Albums, a photo storage site that is integrated with Google +. It offers web-based sharing, photo editing, album organization, and video storage, along with a desktop application for managing your photos.

Picasa Web Users can upload an unlimited number of photos that are 2,048 × 2,048 pixels. For any photos larger than that, you are limited to 1 GB of storage. If you need more storage, you can subscribe to a monthly plan starting at $2.49 for 25 GB.

Uploading photos is easy, and the interface is user-friendly. Unlike a lot of web photo-sharing sites, Picasa does not inundate you with printing services. Picasa supports a variety of file types, including PSD, TGA, and some raw formats.

Looking for tips to get the most out of Picasa? Check out http://picasageeks.com/.

Youtube

YouTube (www.youtube.com) is a website where users can share videos with the public. YouTube contains videos that people have made themselves, excerpts from TV shows, music clips, videos of lectures, TV shows, and movies.

You do not need a YouTube account to view the videos on YouTube, but if you would like to post or share videos, you will need to create one. When you get to the website, at the top of the page, you will see the search bar. A magnifying glass appears to the right of an empty white box. Clicking inside the box allows you to type in search terms. This is a great way to find videos for entertainment or instruction. A lot of users post do-it-yourself videos or instructional how-tos, which are useful if you are trying to learn a new tool. While you are typing, words or sentences will pop up below as suggestions. These suggestions made by YouTube are based on common searches that contain the same letters or words as what you are typing.

You can click one of these suggestions or continue typing your own search terms.

You can share the videos you like on YouTube by clicking the Share this Video link that appears under the videos. This generates a link that you can copy and paste into an e-mail. A handful of icons connect to social media sites (such as Facebook) if you would like to share videos there. If you want to share only a particular part of a video, before copying the link, select the Start At check box. For example, if you want a video to start at 2 minutes and 30 seconds, select the check box and then type "2:30" into the box.

Flickr

Flickr lets you share, store, and organize your photos; it provides easy management and collaboration in one of the largest photo communities. It can be as simple or as complicated as you want it to be. For storage, you can organize your photos into albums (known as "sets") and then further organize those albums into collections. You can share and host tons of your own pictures on Flickr without paying anything for the service. The storage space is limited to 30 MB, but for around $2 per month, you can get unlimited storage and sharing.

On Flickr, you can participate in groups, tag photos, comment on photos, and geotag locations geotagging adds geographical information about where you took the picture to the picture's file). You can even review statistics for your images. Flickr also provides a desktop app, mobile apps, and web-based basic photo editing. You can use Flickr to share your videos as well, making it a one-stop shop for media sharing. On the free account, you are limited to two videos per month. Accompanying Android and iPhone apps are available for the service.

Slideshare

SlideShare (www.slideshare.net) gives you more of a universal hosting service. You can upload PowerPoint, PDF, Keynote, or OpenDocument presentations, infographics, documents, and videos for storage. You can designate the content as public or private. You also can create slide shows of your family photos and share them privately with other members through this site. LinkedIn acquired SlideShare in 2012, and you can link any presentations you upload to your LinkedIn account. If you teach continuing legal education programs or other seminars, this is a great way to share the visual content from your presentations and enhance your LinkedIn portfolio.

You can search through any of the public content for presentations that may be of interest to you. In addition, you can download the content to read at your leisure or reference at a later date.

Plus, you can use SlideShare for your business. For example, you may want to create a visually pleasing presentation for potential new clients, explaining to them how to prepare for an intake interview (i.e., what materials to bring, what to expect). You also can link your SlideShare presentations to your website and showcase your knowledge and expertise in an area of law.

Tips for Travel

One of the truths of life is that when we were young, most of us wanted to travel but did not travel as much as we wanted due to personal or professional obligations, or we simply lacked either the time or the resources or both. Most of us, as we get older, reach a point where we have the freedom and the resources to do more traveling and the inclination to do it. Unfortunately, the older we get, the more likely it is that health issues will intervene and limit our ability to travel after a period of time. Some of us will manage to avoid that situation, but most of us will have to deal with it.

Many of us will have a window of 10 to 15 years when we have the time, the ability, and the good health to allow us to travel significantly. After that, travel will become increasingly difficult. Because most seniors want to do as much traveling as possible, we felt that we should spend some time talking about how to make your travel a bit easier and more comfortable, as well as perhaps a bit less expensive.

Lawyers may spend most of their time in their office, but they also travel both for professional and personal reasons. Travel has become more complicated than it used to be and now often presents serious challenges. In this section, we offer some tips that you may find helpful with respect to personal and professional travels. We anticipate that the included tips may save you time, money, and aggravation when you travel, whether you do so for pleasure or business.

Get a Smartphone and/or a Tablet

Whether you travel a lot or not, you will want to have a smartphone and a tablet. Practically speaking, you will want to have both anyway. If you travel a lot, they morph into indispensable travel companions. In addition to keeping you in touch with your office, family, and friends, they can provide entertainment during your flight (and otherwise); allow you to keep your travel information handy and readily accessible; help you locate the places you want to visit; and provide you with the combined services of a map, tour guide, concierge, translator, currency converter, and travel agent. They also provide a means of keeping a record of your travels via audio recording, video files, photographs, and text.

When it comes to picking a smartphone or a tablet, you have lots of choices. We prefer the Apple products, as they work well together and offer an incredible number of available apps, travel guides, and a vast selection of media. If you do not want to get Apple products for whatever reason, Android-based products hold a strong second place in our estimation. If you opt for Android products, we particularly like Samsung's tablets and, for that matter, Samsung's phones, especially the Galaxy and the Note.

Before you leave, load your devices with the apps that will benefit you most in your work and on your travels, media for entertainment as well as work and, just for the heck of it, throw a few games onto your device.

Oh, one last piece of advice about traveling with smartphones and tablets: if you use cellular data through a US provider while roaming abroad, you will get a hellacious bill. Either limit your web surfing and media streaming to Wi-Fi (see the section of this book respecting security and identity theft to learn about how to do that safely) or get an unlocked device and a local SIM card (one from a provider in the country where you are traveling). Check device compatibility before you go, to make sure you have a device that will work with a local SIM card. You can often get your cellular provider to unlock older devices once you have paid for them. Unlocking the device allows it to work with SIM cards from other providers at home or abroad.

Get an E-Reader

Whether you travel domestically or internationally, you will spend a fair amount of time sitting in airport lounges or on the plane. You will also have downtime during your trip. We always like to have some reading material with us when we travel, but we like to travel light. So, instead of carrying a few books, we carry an e-reader instead. For less than the weight of one book, we can bring along a couple hundred, so whatever mood we find ourselves in, we can find something appropriate to read. Much of the time, you can even get by without the e-reader when you travel because you can add a Kindle or Nook or an iBooks app to your tablet and access most of your electronic library without having to carry the Kindle or Nook. But here's the problem: if you plan on spending time outside in the sun, you will find that your color tablet won't work very well in bright sunlight. The e-Ink technology of the noncolor Kindle and Nook devices remains readable in bright sunlight. For that reason we carry a tablet and an e-Ink reader when we travel.

We prefer the Kindle to the Nook and the Voyage to the other versions of the Kindle e-Ink readers, although the Paper-White is also very good. Amazon has just released the Oasis e-Ink reader as an improvement to the Voyage. Its specs suggest it will give you improved performance over the Voyage. The Voyage is relatively expensive for an e-Ink reader. We have just received ours, but have not seen that the performance boost justifies the cost over the Voyage. It is not clear how much longer Amazon will offer the Voyage; and the Paperwhite is effectively gone (refurbished devices are available for $99). You can buy kindles them at some of the large electronics stores like Best Buy. You can find the Kindle devices at the pop-up Amazon stores at some shopping centers and Nooks at your local Barnes & Noble store. You also can find any and all of the devices online. Amazon.com for Kindle devices and BarnesandNoble.com for Nook devices.

Electronic books generally cost less, always weigh less, and always take up less space than printed versions. You can also adjust print size as displayed for most of them, if you have a problem reading smaller print.

Buy Smart! Fly Smart!

We did some research into which days are the cheapest to fly on and when you should try to book your flight. We learned that the best days to fly (least expensive) generally are Tuesday, Wednesday, and Saturday. The worst (most expensive) are Friday and Sunday. The best buys in airfares usually occur between one and three months prior to departure for domestic fights and five to six months before departure for international flights. Avoid buying a ticket within a week of departure if at all possible, as that is when business travelers get hit with premium prices for last-minute travels. The best time to buy a ticket is on Tuesdays after 3:00 p.m. We are advised that airlines often make fare reductions at 3:00 p.m. on Tuesday afternoons. We know you do not always have the flexibility to buy in these time frames; but when you do, the savings can be substantial.

Do take note of the fact that the information in the preceding paragraph does not mean that you will get inexpensive fares. Airfares have generally increased recently, and airlines have imposed many hidden costs by separating out and charging for things that previously cost nothing, in order to make you believe that you are paying less to fly than you really are. Good examples include food service, checked baggage charges, and charges to go from ultracramped to merely cramped leg space on some flights.

In planning your travel, you should also take into consideration the fact that travel to certain places simply costs more in certain time frames and, with respect to certain holidays, can become extremely expensive. Airfare to a resort destination during the peak of tourist season at that location will always cost more than in shoulder seasons (just before or after the peak season) or in the off-season. Travel around Christmas generally costs more. Domestic travel around Thanksgiving also sees boosted fares. If you want to go to Rio for Carnival, expect to pay much more than you would have to pay at almost any other time of the year. Similarly, expect to pay more if you want to travel to the destination for the next World Cup Finals, Olympics, or Super Bowl around the time of those events.

Use Consolidators

Back in the day, when we planned to travel, we would call our travel agent and tell him or her where and when we wanted to go. The travel agent would arrange the hotel(s) and get the airline tickets. Most travel agents have disappeared, and relatively few of us use travel agents anymore. Most of us have had to make our own travel arrangements or have a secretary make them for us. Once we retire, we likely will have no more secretary and will make our own travel arrangements.

When traveling for pleasure, we can still get some help by going on a tour. If we go on a tour, the tour operator will make the arrangements for us. Going on a tour certainly has some advantages, and many people enjoy traveling that way. Others prefer to avoid tours, knowing that by taking a tour, we trade some of our freedom for convenience.

When we travel on our own, whether for business or pleasure, we have to make our own arrangements. While we may know hotels where we like to stay in cities we regularly frequent or, at least, have gone to in the past, we generally have little information about cities we have not gone to in the past. As the travel industry has changed over the past 15 or 20 years, the industry of consolidators has grown dramatically. Now we can use consolidators to make travel and hotel arrangements for us. The consolidators help us find the right hotel, giving us choices by location, price, and services and often can get us accommodations and transportation at substantially reduced prices.

When it comes to consolidators, you have a large field of providers to choose among. Remember, however, that not all consolidators are created equal. You might want to keep a few points in mind in working with consolidators:

- Before booking with a consolidator you do not know already, check its reputation. Contact the Better Business Bureau; see if it belongs to established trade organizations, such as the United States Air Consolidators Association (USACA), American Society of Travel Agents (ASTA),

International Air Transport Association (IATA), or United States Tour Operators Association (USTOA).

- Let your computer do the walking. Do some comparison shopping. Not all consolidators have the same facilities. Not all consolidators charge the same prices. Make sure that any price quoted to you includes applicable taxes and fees. Sometimes you will do better with short-term promotional fares from the airlines.
- Tickets purchased from consolidators may not qualify for frequent flier mileage. Before you buy, check eligibility with the airline and consolidator.
- Always purchase with a major credit card; that gives you some protection because you can deny payment through your credit card company if problems occur.
- Confirm your reservation both before and after purchasing your ticket.
- Find out what happens if you miss your plane, your flight is canceled, or you need to make a change. Make

sure you obtain clear and accurate information from your consolidator regarding all policies and fees for ticket cancellations, changes, refunds, reticketing, and expiration dates—and then verify these with the airline.

We do not intend to provide you with a complete list of consolidators. We will, however, share with you that we generally use Expedia (www.expedia.com) and Orbitz (www.orbitz.com) for our hotel reservations. Other well-known and respected consolidators include (without limitation) Travelocity (www.travelocity.com), Priceline (www.priceline.com). We particularly like the Kayak (www.kayak.com) site, as it has the facility of allowing you to immediately connect to multiple consolidators and compare the rates that they charge and the packages they have available for your chosen destination. Kayak is a great way to quickly comparison shop.

Most consolidators have websites accessible by browsers from computers and mobile devices. Many also have their own apps for iOS and/or Android devices.

Tripit

Get Tripit! Tripit works like a personal assistant to organize your travel information. You can access it almost anywhere, as it connects to computers through your browser (www.tripit.com), or through most iOS and Android mobile devices through apps or a browser. You can e-mail your flight, hotel, and other confirmations to Tripit, and they will appear in your travel calendar (which you can publish to your primary calendar and share with others). You also can build itineraries that include maps and directions.

You have your choice of three versions: a free version, Tripit Pro, and Tripit for Teams. We have not looked at Tripit for Teams because it is too expensive in our opinion ($29 per month) and does not have as many features as Tripit Pro.

The free version gives you all the basics, but we like the Pro version ($48 per year) better. The Pro version adds several features to the basic package, including automatic sharing, alternate flight location, plus mobile alerts about flight changes and flight price changes. The price change feature justifies the price of admission by itself. Just to give you an idea, I (Jeff) purchased tickets on a major carrier. I sent the flight information to Tripit for inclusion on a travel calendar. About three months later, Tripit sent a notice that the airline had reduced the fare by $200 per person. Tripit recommended returning the tickets and getting new ones at the reduced price. Not a bad strategy, but for the fact that the airline would have charged a fee that would have wiped out much of the savings. Having learned of the reduced fare, however, I called the airline, and we agreed that it would issue a $200 travel credit for each ticket for use in a future ticket purchase.

Flightboard

You can find any number of travel apps for your smartphone or tablet at the iTunes App Store, Google's Play Store, and other locations. Many of them actually can prove helpful to you on your journeys. FlightBoard is one of them. FlightBoard gives you the equivalent of personal airport arrival and departure displays on your smartphone or tablet. You select the airport you want to use, and it gives you current information as to arrivals and departures from that airport. You can narrow the focus from the date by time and airline until you find your flight, and then you can expand the information about your flight.

You choose from over 3,000 airports by touching the word *Airports* in the top left of the display and then typing the city or airport identification code ("San Francisco" and "SFO" both get you there). You can easily and instantly switch from arrivals to departures with the touch of a finger. Note that there is another similar app called Flight Board. It is also a good app, but we prefer this one. This one also won the 2012 Webby Award for Best Travel App.

Flight Update Pro

Flight Update comes in a standard and a pro version. The standard version costs $4.99 at the iTunes App Store. You can get the Pro version directly from the App Store or as an in-app upgrade for $5.99. The pro version gets you push notifications of flight alerts and gate changes, includes nondirect flights when searching by route, and allows you to download flights directly from Tripit, if you link the two accounts. The app provides information about the airport, the weather, the location of your seat in the plane, and the equipment that will be used on your flight. It also gives you detailed information respecting the flight and keeps you up to date on the departure gate.

We have found the app well designed, very useful, and highly functional. As we use Tripit regularly, we particularly like the fact that we can avoid manually entering the details about a flight by linking the account to Tripit and allowing the apps to transfer the data for us. Note that the transfer is one way. You must provide the information to Tripit first if you want the information to transfer to Flight Update Pro. If you send it to Flight Update Pro first, it will not transfer automatically to Tripit, requiring you to take other action to enter it in Tripit's database.

Gate Guru!

We spend more time than we would like sitting in airport waiting rooms. Often we wonder what facilities we will find near our gate. Would it work better to buy something to eat or a cup of coffee before we get to the gate or wait until we get there? If we do not know the airport well, we take potluck, guessing at what we find when we get to the gate. Gate Guru provides inside information. Gate Guru (available for iOS devices at the iTunes App Store) tells you where in the airport you will find what facilities. It tells you where to get magazines, coffee, hamburgers, or hard liquor in the airport. In larger airports, it gives you the option of selecting by gate, by terminal, and by vendor. In addition, the app provides maps of the airport and also offers information as to departing and arriving flights. All of this functionality ought to cost something, but it is a free download from the App Store. Although we trust our own judgment more than CNN's when it comes to evaluating apps, we never object to sharing CNN's opinion when it agrees with our own: CNN rated this a "Top 5 Air Travel App."

Go with GOES!

The Global Online Enrollment System (GOES) lets you clear customs when returning to the United States from international travel more quickly as a "known traveler." With a GOES card, you use an automated kiosk to complete your customs declaration and go through an expedited re-entry process. At least 59 airports offer GOES.

For most people, getting a GOES card is relatively simple: you go online (https://goes-app.cbp.dhs.gov/main/goes), pay a $100 nonrefundable application fee, fill out an application, and wait to hear whether or not you got preliminary approval. If you get preliminary approval, you need to schedule a personal interview so that officials can see you are who you claim to be. Don't wait until the last minute to do this, because although the preliminary approval process results come in relatively quickly, getting an appointment for a personal interview usually takes much longer. You can get the interview only at certain locations, and the waiting period generally runs two or three months. If you persevere, however, you may get in sooner, as often appointments made several months ahead of time sometimes end up creating scheduling problems and get canceled at the last minute. If you check back occasionally, you may find that you can get an appointment in a slot opened as a result of a cancellation on relatively short notice. Sometimes you can get an appointment in a matter of a week or two or, possibly, even a few days. When you go to the appointment, you need to bring your passport with you and some evidence of residence (like a utility bill).

Global Entry also offers some fringe benefits. After approval, if you provide your GOES identification number when you purchase airline tickets, you will get "TSA Pre" approval on your boarding passes when you embark from a US airport. For those unfamiliar with TSA Pre, it saves a fair amount of time and inconvenience during the check-in process. Most airports provide separate lines for TSA Pre customers when you go through security. Those in the TSE Pre line do not have to get undressed, take computers out of briefcases, remove toiletries from suitcases, and then repack everything on the other side of the X-ray machine. You get to leave everything in place, go through, pick it up, and leave. There are some exceptions, however. If you have metal in your pockets, it has to come out; if you have too much metal in your belt buckle or watch or metal in your shoes, you may have to remove them; and if you are wearing a heavy coat, you have to send it through the machine separately (you do not have to remove light jackets, vests, or sweaters). In our experience, it takes us about 25 to 30 percent of the time to get through the security clearance process with TSA Pre by comparison to the standard procedures. A word of warning: if the TSA people see something in your bag that they perceive as suspicious, you still get to wait while they search through its contents and check for gunpowder residue.

Open Table

We have used the Open Table reservation service for several years to help us find the right restaurant and make reservations for our meals. We like it so much that we even use it when we are not traveling. It provides information as to what restaurants you have to choose from in various cities and neighborhoods, the cuisine, the cost, the ambiance, and what other diners have thought about the place. We have found some very nice restaurants using Open Table and, at least so far, it has not led us astray. Open Table does not yet provide information about every city, but it can help you with many metropolitan areas in the United States and (when we last checked) over 20 countries throughout the world. For a complete listing of the geographies covered, check out the Open Table website at www.opentable.com.

Open Table checks available times and dates, and you can schedule your reservation through its website. If you need to change the reservation, it can handle that as well. In addition, whenever you make a reservation through Open Table and then check in at the restaurant, you get Open Table points. You can later redeem the points for a "dining cheque" that you can use to pay your restaurant tab at an Open Table–registered restaurant at a later date. The basic rate is 100 points per reservation, but sometimes you can get a special deal that gets you more. Often 1,000-point tables are available. Check out the site or download the free app for additional details.

Use GPS to Get Around

The smartphones we have recommended (along with many other smartphones and many tablets) all have Global Positioning System (GPS) capabilities. We have had GPS available to us in a variety of devices ranging from mobile phones to dedicated navigation devices in our cars for a number of years. Likely everyone reading this book has some familiarity with GPS navigation devices, and many of you probably have them in your personal cars.

What you may not know is that you can get GPS devices with maps for most major metropolitan areas in the world. You also can get apps that download GPS-based maps onto smartphones and tablets. What you also may not know is that some apps use Internet-based information to help you navigate, whereas others do not. If you use a navigation app that requires Internet information to work, you may run up a large data bill if you use a US-provider-based phone in roaming mode. On the other hand, you can avoid that problem if you use a navigation app that does not require the Internet to work; you download the maps before you leave or use Wi-Fi while on your trip and then use them from your device to translate the GPS information and provide you with location and direction details. If you travel within the United States, this is a much smaller issue, unless you have a very limited cellular data plan.

You can get a number of GPS mapping apps that have downloadable maps that you can keep on your mobile device, avoiding the need to access cloud-based mapping information that will invade your data allowance. Two that we have found particularly useful are the City Walk series (www.GPSmycity.com) and the Ulmon series, both available at the iTunes App Store. The basic software costs nothing, but you pay for downloading maps of your destinations. City Walk also has a lite version of many of its maps that you can get free. These maps lack the detail of the paid versions but will prove functionality for many uses. City Walk has maps for almost 500 cities in the United States and throughout the world. It includes a number of features very helpful for tourists, including self-guided walks. Typical cost for a city's map is $4.99.

Ulmon has iOS and Android apps and many offline maps for you to download onto your device. You can choose from a standard and a Pro version. The standard version costs nothing and comes with free ads. The Pro version costs a few dollars, but you don't get ads with it. Ulmon has fewer maps than City Walk, but for relatively few dollars, you can get unlimited downloads.

Get Your Own Translator

The first time I (Jeff) went to Europe, in 1973, I knew not to drink the tap water in Paris. I carried a bottle of water around with me. It did not dawn on me until a bit too late that the cafés on the Left Bank would use that same tap water to make ice (I learned the hard way why people drink soft drinks warm in Europe). Anyway, to make a long story short, I ordered a Coca-Cola with ice. Two days later I came down with Napoleon's Last Hurrah (my description for what I got; it is a similar ailment to Montezuma's Revenge). As we traveled on the TEE trains from France into Switzerland, I got more and more ill, ultimately spiking a temperature of about 104°F. I even started to hallucinate. When I got to Geneva, I left my bags at the hotel and got directions to the nearest medical clinic.

When I arrived at the clinic, I tried to speak English to the doctor but learned that he spoke no English. He did speak German like a native. Unfortunately, my high school German had left me with virtually no conversational ability. Fortunately, he spoke some French, and I remembered enough of my college French to explain what ailed me. He gave me a couple of wonder drugs (that probably still have not cleared the FDA in the United States), which cured me in a few hours. I learned the hard way the importance of being able to communicate when traveling in other countries. Being able to communicate is not just about finding your way around. It goes beyond finding a restaurant or a particular store. Sometimes it gets far more serious.

While English has grown into a more or less ubiquitous language, you can still find many places to travel (some in the United States) where folks either do not speak English at all, or do not speak it in a way that you can understand it. Unfortunately, we have not found a translator for various versions of English as spoken within the United States, but we have found a number of things to help you get along in many foreign countries when English just does not work.

In the old days, you generally needed to speak a foreign language or have a traveling companion who did in order to get by. Today, technology comes to your assistance, and you can get a variety of apps and devices to help you translate from English to numerous other languages and from numerous other languages to English.

When we travel overseas, we always bring a translator along with us, but nowadays the translator consists of an app for a smartphone or tablet or a stand-alone translator. Many of the translators also utilize speech capabilities, so you can speak or type something in English and they will translate your message to the foreign language of your choice or conversely. Some of the apps we particularly like include Google Translate, Duolingo, and iTranslate. Some are iOS only; others come in both iOS and Android versions.

Take a Good Camera along ... and Use It

Some places you will go to again and again and may not need or even want to take pictures on your trip. Other places will represent a once-in-a-lifetime opportunity, and you will likely want a photographic record. Maybe you don't want to post your pictures on Facebook, but you can still enjoy them yourself and share them with close friends and family.

For some of you, the camera in your smartphone will suffice. In fairness, the cameras in our mobile devices have come a long way and now can take some pretty decent pictures, particularly if the person holding the device understands something about lighting and photographic composition. You can also get any number of apps to help you take better pictures or improve them if you failed to capture exactly the picture you want.

While we often take snapshots or a short movie with our smartphone camera, we recognize that nobody has yet made a smartphone that functions as capably as a good digital still camera or movie camera. If you plan on doing some serious traveling, invest in a good camera. If you are an experienced photographer, you know the advantages of a decent system camera. If you do not want to carry that much equipment, consider getting a high-quality digital camera to slip into your pocket. Such cameras come in small sizes these days, with a range of features suitable for everyone from the rankest amateur to the enthusiast to the professional.

Our favorite high-powered compact camera comes from Sony. Sony released the DSC RX100 several years ago and has upgraded it three times. The most current iteration, the RX100 IV, has some substantial advantages over the earlier models. The earlier models were so good, however, that rather than discontinue them, Sony simply reduced their price and continues to sell them. While we prefer the RX100 IV, we wouldn't refuse to use an RX100 or RX100 II or RX100 III (we actually bought the RX100 when it first came out and recently upgraded to the RX100 III, but still use both). Sony currently lists the RX100 for

$499.99, the RX100 II for $649.99, and the RX100 III for $799.99; but you can get it for less online at a variety of stores. We found the RX100 for under $400.00 on Amazon. The most current model, the RX100 IV, lists for $949.99.

The only disadvantage to the RX100 cameras is that they lack long telephoto capabilities. As a result, depending on where we are traveling, we sometimes take along a second compact camera with a long telephoto lens, such as a Sony DSC-HX50V or a Nikon Coolpix L820. That gives us a backup camera with mega-zoom capability, and it still takes up less space than a system camera. When picking out a camera, remember that you always want optical zoom over digital zoom, and that you want to have an image stabilizer, especially on a mega-zoom camera. Most digital cameras come with built-in flash units. A camera with a hot shoe lets you add a more powerful and more flexible flash unit that gives you more creative capabilities.

Taking the best camera in the world on your trip does no good if you don't pull it out and use it. Your friends and family will want to see some of your pictures, and you will enjoy having them to look back at. Oh, and by the way, you can also use the camera to take great pictures of your grandchildren.

Tips to Protect Your Privacy and Identity

Most of us have heard of the hacking problems that have plagued all manner of businesses as well as some government agencies. Security breaches can result in a loss of confidential and/or proprietary information—an occurrence that can create legal, ethical, financial, social, and other issues for us, personally and professionally.

We also know that individuals have had their personal privacy and security invaded by the bad guys. Seniors have become more ready victims than many other groups for a variety of reasons, including the fact that many of them do not exercise the care and caution that they should with respect to cybersecurity. This is largely due to the fact that they have not taken the time to sufficiently familiarize themselves with appropriate protective measures relating to current technology.

Security, privacy, and ethics have a significant interrelationship when it comes to technology. On a personal level, we all want and need to protect our own information from the bad guys to ensure that we do not become victims of identity theft. On a professional level, attorneys have an ethical obligation to protect client information and the confidentiality of client communications.

Safe: It's Not Just for Sex Anymore!

We hear a lot about safe sex these days, and some seniors really do have to concern themselves with that topic. This book, however, deals with technology, and when we talk about safety in the course of social intercourse, our attention turns to e-mail. So, in keeping with the theme, we will give you a few prophylactic measures to help you protect yourself when engaging in e-mailing.

While seniors generally have more life experience than youngers, they generally use e-mail less often and tend to have less familiarity with computer technology and the Internet. To help you out in dealing with e-mail, we have come up with a few tips to help keep you safe:

- **Watch out for strangers!** You may remember warning your children not to talk to strangers. Well, take some of your own advice. Beware of e-mail from unknown sources. Not all e-mail comes from reputable places.

Exercise caution in dealing with
e-mail from people you do not know.

- **Beware the spammer's talk!** Exercise caution in dealing with peculiar
  e-mails from people you do know.
  The amount of spam that we see
  has reached alarming proportions.
  Often someone you know has had
  his or her e-mail account security
  breached, and one of the bad guys
  has sent e-mail to your friend's contacts (you) in furtherance of a scam
  or with malware attached to it.
  One of our favorites tells a tale of
  woe from a friend who has traveled
  abroad and had his wallet and passport stolen, and now writes beseeching you to send some money.

- **Don't click that link!** If you get an
  e-mail purporting to be from your
  bank, the government, or a vendor
  you recognize telling you about some
  problem and providing you with a
  link to use to respond with required
  information or clear up a problem
  with your account, don't click the
  link! Chances are high that the message is not from that vendor at all,

but from spammers seeking to obtain personal information to enable them to access your accounts or steal your identity. Instead, independently access the vendor's website directly or call the vendor to verify whether or not you need to fix something with your account.

When in Doubt, Throw it Out!

This tip could have been a fourth piece of advice under e-mail safety, but we thought its importance required separate treatment. E-mail attachments can carry all kinds of viruses, malware, and other problems. If you get an e-mail that comes from an unknown source or that just does not seem quite right, suggesting you open an attachment, just say "NO"! Think of the attachment as a package of stale dated smoked salmon—not something you want to get into because you just don't know how much damage it can cause. As Johnnie Cochran might have said, if asked to come up with an appropriate rule for dealing with stale dated smoked salmon or questionable e-mail attachments:

WHEN IN DOUBT, THROW IT OUT!

Password-Protect Your Devices

Smartphones, tablets, and computers all allow you to create an electronic locking mechanism to protect against improper access. These mechanisms run the gamut from biometric scanning to numeric codes to more complex alphanumeric and alpha-numeric–symbolic passwords.

Unfortunately, you have the option of turning off the electronic protection. Worse yet, some devices come with the default set to the off position. We think you should always password-protect your computers, tablets, and smartphones. It would help if manufacturers set the default to pass-word protection and required you to select a password as part of the setup process (some do and we applaud that approach). Even a four-digit password helps, but you don't have to settle for that. If you go to the settings on most devices, you can acti-vate longer passwords and build a longer, stronger password using a combination of different types of characters.

Do Not Use the Same Password for Everything

More and more service providers impose password requirements on us. Banks have passwords for accessing our accounts. We need a password to log in to our Westlaw or Lexis accounts. We need a password to log in to our iCloud accounts. We need a password for Dropbox. We need a password for pretty much everything these days. If you listen to us, you even need one for your smartphone, tablet, and computer. The use of passwords to access everything tends to make some people want to choose one easily remembered password and to use it for most, if not all, accounts. We cannot do that, in part because not all passwords have the same construction requirements. Some require numeric only, some require alpha and numeric characters, some require both, some require different numbers of characters, and some require the use of symbols in addition to alphanumeric characters.

Even if someone passed a law that said all password requirements had to have identical characteristics, we would not want to use the same password for accessing all of our information, accounts, and devices. Simply put, if you have a single password for everything and someone gets that password, that person has the keys to the kingdom. Use a different password for each account that contains important information. Some accounts do not contain important or confidential information. While it would be better to have unique passwords for all accounts, if you really want to use the same password for multiple accounts, limit that exercise to the accounts that do not contain important or confidential information. Consider all bank accounts, accounts that allow you to purchase something, or those that will hold any private, personal, confidential, or client information important enough to have their own special and unique password.

By the way, you should not pick a password and use it on the account forever. You should change your passwords every once in a while (not less than once every six months). If you suspect a data breach, you should immediately change your passwords on all affected accounts.

Use Strong Passwords

Using a simple password makes it easier for the bad guys to determine the password and access information, files, and devices. Stay away from simple or weak passwords, and do not use the same password for multiple accounts. If you have password requirements for access to accounts that do not acquire information you legally must or simply want to keep confidential, you can safely duplicate password use for such accounts. If you do that, however, do not also use the same password for anything that can access confidential or private information. Here are some guidelines for passwords:

Weak passwords (the ones you don't want to use):

- Some examples of weak passwords: "password", "12345", "abcde".
- Anything easily associated with you, such as your name, initials, birth-date, address, and so on.

Rules to build strong passwords (the ones you want to use):

- Random characters work well, but you don't have to go that way (random characters are hard to remember).
- Mix alphanumeric–symbolic characters and use both capital and lower case letters.
- Use at least eight characters in your passwords.
- Pass phrases beat passwords (longer beats shorter).
- Even with a longer pass phrase, mix alphanumeric–symbolic characters and capital/lowercase letters.
- Here's an example of a passphrase: "666IsTheNumberoftheBeast!!!"

Check Your Password Strength

You can find software that will check the strength of your password against the strength of password-cracking software. We like that for all passwords, no matter how you generate them. This software is particularly helpful when you create your own using nonrandomly selected characters.

How Secure Is My Password (http://howsecureismypassword.com) provides an estimate as to how long contemporary password-cracking software would require to crack your password. When we tested a password that we created, we found the results (4,000 years) a bit surprising. While the time required certainly gave us a sense of confidence in the security of our password choice, we honestly believe that anything over 1,000 years is just bragging.

Keep Your Passwords Secure

No matter how good a job you do choosing a strong password, the effort amounts to nothing if you do not appropriately secure your password. Over the years we have seen all manners of storing passwords, some better than others. Some password storage we have seen is so bad that it is most charitably described as negligent. Among the really bad ideas we have seen:

- Writing the password on a sticky note and sticking it to a desk or computer monitor.
- Writing the password on a 3- by 5-inch card or a piece of paper and jamming it into the side of a desk blotter.
- Pinning the password to a corkboard on the wall of a secretary's cubicle.

Think of each step in cybersecurity as a link in a chain. Keeping your passwords secure often proves the weakest link in the chain. We all know what happens when a chain has a weak link....

Use Biometric Security

More and more companies have come to the conclusion that biometric devices provide the best means of security and access. Although technically not a password, these devices function similarly in terms of access to devices and files.

Biometric devices usually use fingerprint scanners, although some of the more sophisticated versions use retinal scans. Biometric devices sometimes come attached to a device, such as part of the DNA of the iPhone and the newer iPads, or as a fingerprint scanner built into a laptop computer or a keyboard. Other devices come separately and connect upon attachment to the computer, often via a USB port.

We have found that the newer biometric devices (mostly fingerprint scanners) work fairly reliably. All of the biometric security devices we have tried offer a backup option of password entry if the biometrics don't allow access for some reason. Consequently, we have become advocates of using them when they are available. Until then (and even afterward in terms of a backup password), keep in mind the guidelines we suggested for strong passwords.

Use a Password Generator

As our lives become more complex and our Internet dependence more complete, we end up with an ever-increasing number of passwords required to access our accounts, devices, and information.

We need to use strong passwords to protect confidential information and should not duplicate use of the same passwords for different accounts. The result is an ever-growing list of passwords. The longer the list, the harder it becomes to remember all the passwords. You can get some help on that front, however. Many programs securely store your passwords for you, allowing you to retrieve them. That way, you have to remember only the password to get into the device and the password for the security program. Most of these programs not only store passwords for you but also can help you generate secure passwords (most of which you would not remember without the program's help). A number of the programs also store confidential data, such as credit card and account numbers for you.

Many of these programs allow installation on numerous devices. They can even move information such as your passwords from one entry point to all the devices connected to your account, making them incredibly useful and easy to use. We have found several programs that we like, including 1Password by Agilebits (www.agilebits .com). You can get versions for computers, tablets, and smartphones. While we like and use these systems, be careful with them. Ultimately, they mean that everything comes down to a single password that opens up the information to all your accounts. Accordingly, if you choose to use one, pick a very strong password for it and make very sure to keep that password secure.

Avoid Public Wi-Fi

Public Wi-Fi connections expose you to greater risk than secure private connections. Public hotspots include the free connections at Starbucks and the connections (free or paid for) at hotels, on airplanes, and the like. A public Wi-Fi connection presents a shared network that allows strangers to potentially access your electronics joined on the shared network.

Protect yourself. Protect your clients. Protect your data. Keep away from public Wi-Fi. If you find yourself in a situation where you have to use public WiFi (such as on a plane or while traveling), run your information through a VPN (Virtual Private Network). A VPN provides a secure tunnel through the Internet to protect your information. You can find VPN apps to make this task easier.

Keep Your Software Up to Date

Many people think that if their computer or mobile device works, they don't need to update the operating system or program software. WRONG! The bad guys constantly look for weaknesses in software and operating systems that will enable them to access computers to wreak their havoc. Software developers issue updates for a variety of reasons. Sometimes the updates cure problems in the operation of the software, sometimes they add new features, and sometimes they close security holes that enable the bad guys to get into computers and/or mobile devices.

Regularly checking for and installing updates can provide new features for you and also enhance the security of your system and device.

We sympathize with those of you who hesitate to mess with something that works and prefer to operate on the theory that "if it ain't broke, don't fix it." We have been burned on more than one occasion by a prematurely released update that proved less than ready for prime-time. The good news is that we have had no problems with the overwhelming majority of the updates that we have installed from responsible and well-established vendors. We won't endeavor to list all the vendors from whom we have installed software updates with and without problems, as we have not maintained those records. We will tell you that we have had issues with installations from all major vendors including Microsoft and Apple. That said, we continue to recommend that you keep your software (and, in particular, your operating systems) current, especially with respect to security issues.

We do, however, offer one suggestion in the interest of self-preservation: when a new fix comes out, you do not have to install it before anyone else. Let someone else test it first. Wait a few days and check to see if people have reported any problems with it. Then you can decide to move forward or wait. There have been times when that approach saved considerable trouble as a vendor released an update, discovered an issue, and then released a fix for it shortly thereafter. By waiting a few days, we learned of and avoided the problems of the initial iteration, getting the updated version within a week of the release of the initial one.

Similarly, when a company stops supporting a particular version of its operating system or software, stop using it. We recently had that experience when Microsoft announced that it would no longer support Windows XP. That meant that it would not offer any new corrections for vulnerability problems. We immediately recommended that people stop using XP, even though they liked it and it worked for them.

Help Prevent Identity Theft: Use Apple Pay

If you have a newer iPhone (5s or later running iOS 8 or 9), you can connect many of your credit cards to the Apple Pay system. To the extent that you can use Apple Pay, you reduce your exposure to identity theft and credit card number theft. The system provides greater security than the physical card, and you can have several of them connected to your Apple Pay account. Note that you can use Apple Pay with any iOS device that has a fingerprint reader, including all recent iPads. Apple has advised that Apple Pay will also work with the Apple Watch. You get Apple Pay through the Wallet App. In addition to credit cards, you can also add airline boarding passes and event tickets to your account.

Apple Pay's security results from several factors. Apple Pay does not work until you verify that you are you by using your finger- or thumb print. Once you have done that, Apple Pay processes the transaction. In processing it, Apple Pay does not transmit your full account number in connection with transactions. Rather, it creates a new number keyed exclusively to your device and transmits that number. Apple does not store your account information on its computers.

While we like Apple Pay very much, we do want to make sure that you understand its limitations. First of all, not all banks coordinate with Apple Pay. If your bank does not work with Apple Pay, you won't be able to get your credit card issued by that bank on the Apple Pay account. Second, some banks allow only some credit cards to work with Apple Pay. For example, at this time, Chase allows personal credit cards to connect to Apple Pay, but it does not allow business accounts to connect. Third, you can get away without carrying most of your cards, but you should carry at least one physical card because not all vendors accept Apple Pay. It requires a reader that not all vendors have acquired as yet.

In the aftermath of Apple Pay's release, Google, Samsung, and others offered their own iterations of electronic payment using smart devices as vehicles for payment. It is hard to say which has achieved the best acceptance, but we see more and more stores accepting electronic payments. Likely, this will go the way of the VHS/beta war and one will win out and everyone will use it for a while. We just don't know which one yet.

Technology and Health

You have likely heard it said that you can tell when you find yourself in a room full of seniors because the primary topic of conversation turns to their health. While younger people have grown more conscious of their health and started to pay more attention to fitness, the fact remains that, as a general rule, the older you get, the more conscious you become of your health and health issues. Technology respecting health care and fitness continues to grow at least as fast as any other area of technology. Accordingly, we felt that we could not call our book on technology tips for seniors complete without including a section on health and technology.

Whether your interest stems from curiosity, a desire to improve your general health, or the fact that you have acquired an illness of some sort that requires monitoring, the new technologies in the health-care field will likely offer you some assistance. Those that most of us concern ourselves with relate to vision, hearing, blood pressure, blood sugar, and general fitness. The general fitness category includes how much you eat, what you eat, how much activity you get, and what type of activity you get.

Although we don't generally think of age as a disability in the same way that we view other conditions, we do recognize that it often imposes physical and mental limitations on people. These limitations include things that we regularly perceive as disabilities, such as impairment of vision, hearing, memory, and mobility—almost all of which will affect most of us as we age. Some people may never suffer from such limiting conditions, but the advancements that make things better for those who do can also benefit those who don't have serious issues. Accordingly, advances in mobile technology that can mitigate these conditions have direct and personal significance to all of us.

Activity Trackers

Back in the day, most of us considered a pedometer pretty fancy tech. We could carry it around, and it would count our steps. Today's pedometer is part of a much more complex and powerful activity tracker that can not only count steps but also use GPS to more accurately analyze how far you traveled; keep track of walking, running, and other exercise and activities to calculate how many calories you have burned; and record the quality of your sleep (how long, how restless, how many times you woke up). Some of the most recently released activity trackers can also tell you how many flights of stairs you climbed during the day, give you a running record of your pulse, and even tell you the time and date.

The really high-tech versions can connect to your smartphone, laptop, or computer; feed the information into apps on those devices; let you know when you get a phone call or a text message; and the beat goes on....

Does everyone need all that information? Probably not. Does it help to have it? Likely, it does. For anyone looking to keep fit or get fit, tracking calories in and out tends to help the process along. If you know you should walk 8,000 steps in a day, it helps to not have to count each one as you take it. You will likely pay more attention to doing it if you do not have to count yourself. Moreover, seeing that you have only walked 1,500 steps might induce you to take the dog for a walk to add another few thousand steps to your total for the day. It all has to start somewhere.

Speaking of starting, these devices do no good in your dresser drawer. If you get one, you have to put it on. Once you put it on, you need to keep it on. We have seen survey results showing that approximately a third of the people who start with activity trackers stop within six months. You need to persevere to benefit.

Do bear in mind that you should view these devices as providing you with an estimation of calories consumed and burned. They are not perfectly accurate, and you should not rely on them as though they accurately record everything. That said, they seem to do a pretty good job and provide useful information.

You have a lot of choices when it comes to picking an activity tracker. In truth, most of them still look pretty clunky, but lately we have seen some of the manufacturers moving toward less clunky-looking devices. A few have even started the movement toward a fashion statement. Unfortunately, the high-fashion versions usually have prices to match, but you can certainly get by with a less fashionable and less expensive model.

We both have favored the Fitbit devices, finding them useful, reliable, and easy to use. Both of us used the Fitbit Flex for the last year or so. It does not look high fashion, but it works. Last year Fitbit released newer, fancier, more expensive versions, the Surge and the Charge, which did more things but unfortunately looked no more stylish. Those remain available. This year, newer, and more stylish versions came out: the Blaze and the Alta. You can compare the features in detail at www.fitbit.com.

Speaking of jewelry, the Apple Watch does far more than just track activities (but it does that too). Apple designed it to handle electronic payments, control music on your iPhone, let you know about phone calls and text messages, display your calendar, remotely use the camera on your iPhone, and on and on. You can check out all the features at www.apple.com.

Apple has tried to position the Watch not only as a tech partner for your smartphone and tablet, but also as a fashion statement. All of the Apple Watches do exactly the same thing. Each of the three lines uses different materials and has different bands. The least expensive, the Watch Sport, costs $299 to $349, depending on your choice of band and size. The intermediate range, called Watch, starts at $649 and goes to $1,049, with the choice of size and band determining the final cost. A special edition of the Watch in collaboration with the designer Hermès runs $1,150 to $1,500. The most expensive, the Watch Edition, comes with a solid gold case and costs between $10,000 and $17,000; again, size and band choice will fix the final price (at least until somebody gets the bright idea to add gemstones to the package and really get the price up into the stratosphere).

The Apple watch offers many interesting features but has the disadvantage of not measuring sleep cycles, likely due to the fact that it requires daily recharging and the paradigm call for you to wear it all day and recharge it during the night while you sleep.

This Ain't Your Grandpa's Ear Trumpet!

As we get older, many of us will lose auditory acuity. In most cases, the loss is not disabling, but it can significantly impact your personal life as well as your professional activities. Hearing loss can lead to misunderstanding statements made by judges, witnesses, other attorneys, and clients. It can also create socially embarrassing situations.

Hearing aids have become unobtrusive in recent years; in many cases, they are virtually undetectable. Unfortunately, the smaller and more-difficult-to-detect hearing aids generally cost much more than the larger ones and often are not covered by medical insurance.

High-grade nonprescription sound amplifiers, some of which are very diminutive in size, may be the solution for some. Generally lacking the adjustability of a prescription hearing aid, nonprescription sound amplifiers are not suitable for correction of serious hearing losses. For those with relatively minor hearing impairment, however, they may prove just the thing, at a fraction of the cost of prescription hearing aids.

The more recent versions of hearing aids come in two basic styles: those that fit completely into the ear canal and those that rest behind the ear and pipe sound into the ear through a practically invisible plastic tube. Although both work well, some styles work better for people with certain types of hearing loss.

Some hearing aids have Bluetooth technology, either through the use of a separate intermediate device or, with some of the newer models, directly into the hearing aids themselves (a situation we prefer). Bluetooth technology lets you stream music from your Bluetooth-equipped computers, tablets, telephones, or music players and answer telephone calls through the hearing aids, saving you the cost of acquiring a separate Bluetooth headset for your smartphone and the inconvenience of wearing it.

An article titled "Hearing Loss in Older Adults" published by *American Family Physician* in June 2012 noted that 28 million adult Americans have hearing loss, making it the third most common health problem in older adults. The article states that one-third of adults between 61 and 70 years old and more than 80 percent of those over 85 suffer from hearing loss. A study published by the National Institute on Deafness and Other Communication Disorders in 2014 reported that only 20 percent of those who could benefit from a hearing aid actually wear one.

Hearing deficits sneak up on you. You don't notice them because you don't realize the sound you lose at first. Unlike vision problems, with hearing problems, you may not notice the issue until it becomes serious. Early signs of hearing loss include difficulty hearing and understanding people in crowded environments like restaurants or having to turn up the telephone, music, and television speaker volume. Ultimately, others may start to complain that you have hearing problems or that you need to turn down the television. Don't wait for friends and family to tell you that you have a hearing problem. See an audiologist and have a hearing test to determine if you have hearing loss and learn what you can do to mitigate it.

Keep Track of What You Eat

A myriad of apps exist to help you with your health. One of our favorites, LOSE IT!, works on smartphones, tablets, and computers, allowing you to input information using any of those devices and check your status on any of them. Since the app stores the information in the cloud, it will also sync the data among all your Internet-connected devices on which you have installed the app.

The app gives you lots of ways to find the right food to enter: by grocery store identification, by restaurant menu, by manually entering the specific information about your food (from the label of a product), and (our favorite) by scanning the bar code on the package label so that you do not have to look it up or guess. It uses the camera in your smartphone or tablet to scan the bar code and then looks it up on the Internet. That particular feature does not exist in the computer version but works very well in the app version.

The program figures out how many calories you should eat and lets you know how you are doing each day. It also keeps track of your weight and lets you know how you are doing toward reaching any goal weight you have set for yourself. It can even calculate how long it should take you to reach your goal weight.

One of the other interesting things about this particular app is that in setting up the apps that track health information for research purposes, which connect to the Apple Watch, we discovered that those apps also connect to LOSE IT! Once connected, they move the information across not only your devices, but across apps within the devices, allowing them to share data. The LOSE IT! app costs nothing, but you need an account to use it and store your information. The basic account also costs nothing, but for $29.99 a year you can get the premium subscription, which provides you more detailed information.

The app also coordinates with the data from Fitbit devices. Check it out at www. fitbit.com, at the iTunes App Store, or at Google's Play Store.

Track Your Glucose

According to the American Diabetes Association website: "Diabetes disproportionately affects older adults. Approximately 25% of Americans over the age of 60 years have diabetes, and aging of the U.S. population is widely acknowledged as one of the drivers of the diabetes epidemic" (www.diabetes.org/).

If you have diabetes, in addition to keeping track of your food intake, exercise, and how you feel each day, you also need to keep a record of your blood glucose levels. Many apps already exist in this niche, and hardware is rapidly marching along as well. Let us tell you about a couple that we really like.

As part of the health tech rolling out in connection with the Apple Watch, an app called Glucose Success connects to LOSE IT! and to your wearable activity tracker (whether the Apple Watch or Fitbit). It coordinates data from several sources, reporting it anonymously for research purposes and making it available to you. As part of the process, it asks you to input certain information each day: weight (manually entered), blood glucose level (manually entered from a finger-stick reading), information as to the condition of your feet (often a problem for diabetics), the amount of time you slept the previous night, and your perception of your health. If you want to go back and see what your blood glucose level was last week or last month, it holds that data for you.

Another excellent app for tracking blood glucose is DiabetesPal. It lets you manually add information from a finger-stick reading off any glucose meter but automatically transmits the data if you use one of its wireless Telcare blood glucose meters. We especially like the way this app is structured, as it lets you enter several readings a day, and calculates statistical averages of your blood glucose over time and at different times of day. And, certainly not least, it compiles a report of your readings and stats for a 7-, 14-, 30-, or 90-day period and e-mails them so that you can share them with your physician. You can get it for iOS or Android devices in the iTunes App Store or Google's Play Store.

Is There a Doctor in the House?

Most of us grew up with a family doctor who took care of our siblings and us (or possibly our entire family). Back in those days, doctors even made house calls. As you know, the world of medical care has changed dramatically over the past 50 years. Today, doctors don't generally make house calls, everyone seems to specialize, and almost nobody does general family practice. Instead, most physicians have joined relatively large medical groups that provide administrative staffing whose sole purpose frequently appears to be preventing patients from communicating directly with their physicians. Often patients find that they have to wait what they perceive as unreasonably long periods for an appointment with their doctors.

The Internet has brought many interesting capabilities and services to us. One of those services is the ability to have an e-visit with a qualified physician on short notice. All you need is an Internet connection, a device with a browser, and a credit card to have a virtual house call at almost any time, day or night.

You have an increasing number of providers to choose from. One that we learned about from AARP is MDLIVE (www.mdlive.com). This service recently released an app to make it even easier to access a physician. The app comes in both iOS and Android versions (available at the iTunes App Store and Google's Play Store). MDLIVE has board-certified physicians and licensed therapists on call any time (24/7 including holidays) using your computer or a mobile device. It charges $49 for a virtual visit of 12 minutes. According to the website, the service has 2,300 doctors and therapists on its roster, over 90 percent of its customers rate the experience as excellent or good, and 94 percent of patient medical issues are resolved by its doctors through the virtual visit.

To get started, go to www.mdlive.com and sign up for a free account. You do not pay anything for the account; you pay only when you have a virtual visit with a physician or therapist. The physicians and therapists dispense advice and, when necessary and appropriate, provide prescriptions for required medications. They send the prescription to the pharmacy of your choice for fulfillment. As a general rule, they issue prescriptions only for short time periods (up to 30 days). They make a point of noting that the service is not designed to provide long-term care or to serve as a primary physician. It is designed to handle nonemergency, short-term medical needs only. Please note that some states impose limitations on the available services. The website contains information as to the limitations.

Other companies providing similar services include AppMedicine (www.appmedicine.com) and Doctor on Demand (www.doctorondemand.com). Please note that the authors are not medical doctors and take no responsibility for the medical diagnoses provided through these sites. We are simply advising you that they exist, should you care to use them.

Here's to Your Health

With the release of iOS 8, Apple introduced its Health Kit. It remains a part of iOS 9. The Health Kit includes an app simply called Health. Health connects with other apps to exchange information and accepts information from several activity trackers (including the Apple Watch). The Health app can collect and store information, providing you with an easily understood graphical representation of the data. That makes it a fairly useful app to have but does not make it stand out from a number of apps that can do similar things (although the graphic representations are nice).

The Health app also lets you to store a significant amount of information about your health, including applicable medical conditions and a record of all the medications you take. Again, this capability does not make it better than other apps that can do the same thing, but that it does that in addition to the sharing and analyzing of other health information begins to make it stand out.

The Health app provides the capability to create a medical ID that includes emergency contact information, your history, and medications. Again, Health joins other apps in providing that functionality, but again that it does that in addition to the other features pushes it toward the lead.

Using the app is easy. Tap on the app to open it. Complete the information and save it. Tap the button to set up a medical ID and fill it in; then save that.

Health can make your emergency information available to others, even with the lock screen on. Accessing it is easy. When the device is locked, you can slide the lock screen image away to get to the passcode entry requirement. On the bottom of the screen, you will see the word *Emergency*. Touch that and then touch the medical ID link on the bottom left of the passcode entry screen to open your medical ID. It displays the information you have put in, while still leaving your iPhone locked. If you get seriously ill or injured, that information could save your life.

Additionally, Health allows you to generate a summary of the data. You can use that information for your own reference or print it or e-mail it and share it with your physician(s).

We have not found any other app that does all of the things this app does or that does them any better. We would recommend this app to you even if you had to pay a few dollars for it. We think it would be worth the cost. How much better is it that we can tell you it costs nothing? Apple gives it to you as part of the iOS. (Yay, Apple!) Android users, you are out of luck; this app works only on the iOS devices running iOS 8.0 or later.

Supersize That!

OK, the fast-food places gave supersizing a bad name. Supersizing there might impair your health if you do it often enough. For many of us who have passed age 45, however, presbyopia (aka "middle-aged vision") has set in, and we discover that our arms lack the reach to allow us to focus on small (or what we used to consider normal sized) print in books, on menus, or in documents. While that may mean you should look into LASIK eye surgery to repair your vision or at least get reading glasses, sometimes that won't solve the problem. Even those of us who have reading glasses sometimes run into difficulty reading small print, especially things like the identification codes printed with light-colored ink in microscopic sizes on SIM cards or other things. When I (Jeff) first encountered this problem, I started to carry a magnifier with me to use when reading glasses just did not do the trick. That worked fine, except when I forgot to take the magnifier with me.

Smartphones to the rescue! Most of us almost never go anywhere without our smartphones. You can get apps that use the smartphone's camera to magnify print or objects, making them easier for you to see. Two examples that we like a lot on the iPhone are EyeReader ($1.99) and Reading Assistant ($.99); they can magnify objects to several times their actual size, making it easier to read print or see very small objects. Using a stand to free up both hands can also make it much easier to do things like thread a needle, loosen (or tighten) a very small screw, or inspect the condition of small objects. Both of those apps work well with iPhones, the iPad, and the iPad Mini.

Those of you on Android devices don't need to feel left out. While these two apps don't work on your devices, Google's Play Store has several apps that do the same thing. Examples include Magnifier, Magnifying Glass, and Smart Reading Glasses. All come free, and since turnabout is fair play, none of them work on the iOS devices.

You can also get the same results on most smartphones with the camera working by itself. Many of them allow you to zoom in on images, even without taking a picture.

You can also take a picture and zoom in on it when viewing it. We have found that capability useful when we need to refer to something repeatedly.

Even if you do not suffer from presby-opia, having one of these tools available comes in handy when you have to read something really small.

It's My Health and I'll Look If I Want to!

One of the new developments in health tech is that many medical practice groups and laboratories have adopted technology and set up websites and smartphone/tablet apps that (1) let you communicate with your health-care professionals by e-mail; (2) let you access your own medical records, prescription records, and test results directly; (3) schedule or change appointments without having to call the office and wait on hold; and (4) request prescription renewals.

Not all medical groups and laboratories have this technology yet. We have tried them out (our doctors and the laboratory we use have these facilities). The process saves considerable time and frustration. It also allows us to communicate directly with our physician (albeit by e-mail), rather than have to leave messages with clerical staff that may or may not accurately deliver the information to the doctor.

We will not give you recommendations as to particular apps because we have experience only with our own doctors and their medical groups and the laboratories we normally use. We would not give up a physician we liked because the doctor did not have this type of access. However, if we were looking for a new doctor or a laboratory to provide services and care to us, we would let this facility serve as the tipping point if we found two or more substantially equally qualified physicians in a search for a new physician, but only one of them offered this type of connectivity and contact.

If you have a doctor with this facility available, try it out. We think you will want to continue to use it as a result of the convenience it affords you.

Helpful Emergency Tip!

Many laboratories and physicians groups have adopted the Internet into their practice, making it possible for patients to communicate with doctors and obtain laboratory results. Some of those setups also allow you to download some or all of your medical records. Once you have done that, you should get a small USB flash drive, put it on your keychain, and add a copy of your medical records. You should make sure that the records include a list of all medications that you take. It would probably also prove helpful to include a PDF copy of a signed current medical power of attorney to help you and treating physicians in case of an accident, illness, or emergency. You might want to mark one side of it with something to let medical personnel know that it contains medical information, in case you have lost consciousness. A caduceus works very well for that purpose. This tip might just save your life one day.

Other Useful Tips

In creating this collection of tips, we found some that we wanted to share with you, but they did not fit well into the categories we used to organize the tips. This section consists of assorted and sundry tips that we think you may find valuable, useful, helpful, entertaining, and/or interesting.

Grid-It

Memory glitches can happen to anyone, but lots of tools can assist you with remembering things. If you travel with your technology a lot, check out GRID-IT. If you are a visual person, then a system like GRID-IT can help prevent you from absent-mindedly forgetting to pack an important cable or device when you go somewhere. If you don't need that help, GRID-IT will still help you keep your electronics and attachments organized and together so that you can easily find them.

GRID-IT is a rubberized, woven-elastic object retention system designed to help to organize and easily locate your gadgets and cables. It fits neatly inside bags and briefcases to keep you organized on the go. The system holds thumb drives, spare batteries, business card cases, charging and connector cables, cameras, reading glasses—almost anything you can think of. The elastic bands hold the items firmly in place, and the rubberized backing prevents them from sliding around. If the contents you are organizing are fragile, you should place the organizer in a padded pocket, but if the goal is solely organization of small electronics devices and cables, this system has it all.

Use Electronic Business Cards

If you use Microsoft Outlook, you can easily create an electronic business card. When you attach an electronic business card to your e-mail, recipients can right-click the card in the signature block (or right-click the .vcf file attachment) to save it directly to their contacts list. To start, open Outlook and a blank e-mail. Then you can choose to create a signature or choose an existing signature to modify. From here, you can select to include a business card in the signature.

If you would like some help creating your electronic business card, you can download templates through Microsoft at http://office.microsoft.com/en-us/templates/results.aspx?ctags = CT010253053&CTT = 5&origin = HA010065086.

You can even add backgrounds and images to your electronic business card. To avoid distortion, you should select a background image about the same size as the electronic business card itself (around 248 pixels by 148 pixels). Once you have the image sized appropriately, use the following steps to complete your task:

1. In an open contact, double-click the Electronic Business Card.
2. In the Edit Business Card dialog box, click Change in the Card Design section.
3. Locate the picture that you want to use for the background, and then double-click it.
4. Next to Layout, select Background Image.
5. Click OK.
6. Click Save and Close.

Harness the Power of Technology in Your Disaster Plan

It is important to keep in mind at any age that those who fail to plan, plan to fail. You may have heard the adage "it wasn't raining when Noah built the ark." Without going into religion, the adage sends a clear message; you should plan for disaster before the disaster occurs. Disasters come in many forms: natural disasters (storms, floods, fires, earthquakes), terrorist attacks, and even power outages. Disasters, whether natural or man-made, can cause a devastating personal toll and also create far-reaching business implications.

1. Develop a Disaster Recovery Plan for Your Personnel

First, identify a disaster recovery manager. If you are a solo running a lean operation, then you likely get that job. If possible, you should identify a backup for the disaster recovery manager. You should commit your disaster recovery plan to writing and keep it somewhere your managers can access it off-site in case of emergency. The plan needs to include contact information, including home phone numbers and cell phone numbers for all critical personnel. You may not be able to count on firm e-mail accounts if your server is out of commission. If you rent office space, you may be locked out pending a building inspection. Your recovery plan needs to include the contact information for building management to keep abreast of the latest developments. Designate a method of disseminating information, whether it will be by telephone call, a central call-in number your firm can use, or maybe personal e-mails (if so, you need to keep an updated directory that your disaster recovery manager can access off-site). Your disaster recovery manager needs to identify a point of operations; it may be an off-site location, or perhaps individuals will work from home until building access is possible.

2. It Pays to Be a Mobile Lawyer

We have written several pieces on mobile lawyering, but you will notice that the tools you use as a mobile lawyer can also make disaster recovery easier. As a mobile lawyer, you use tools enabling you to practice almost anywhere, such as a cloud storage system, remote backup of your crucial documents, or a cloud-based phone system such as RingCentral or Google Voice. These same services can play a crucial role in your disaster recovery, substantially shortening your downtime. Look at how these mobile tools can integrate into your disaster recovery plan.

3. You Need a Disaster Recovery Plan for Your Data

The plan could be a cloud-based backup system or a personal backup system. Keep in mind that the disaster affecting your office could also affect your home. You should have more geographic diversity than just your home and office. If you find yourself in the wake of a disaster without a data recovery plan, you may want to start by contacting a data recovery expert in your area.

4. Inform Your Clients, Adversaries, and the Courts of the Disaster and Your Current Position in the Road to Recovery

As Model Rule 1.4 points out, "[a] lawyer must be able to reasonably consult with a

client, including keeping the client reasonably informed and promptly complying
with reasonable requests for information."
Not all clients or courts will be sympa-
thetic, but you likely already have an idea
of which ones will not. You may be able to
forward calls to a remote receptionist area
to receive any incoming calls for you. This
solution allows you to keep a line of communication open for your business while
you organize and regroup.

Outsource Typing

You can find a number of good transcription services to facilitate your work. As your practice grows, outsourcing typing may prove less costly than employing a secretary, at least until your workload hits a certain level. Rather than jump in to the hiring process, you can use any dictation equipment you are comfortable with and send in your files for transcription. Most of these services provide high-quality work with a fast turnaround time. When shopping for a service, look for one that will give you 24-hour or better turnaround time. You should also look for a service that will take your forms and use them as models for your work. For most services, you can easily transport files by e-mail or upload.

You have many choices when it comes to such services. Issues to consider as bases for differentiation include the following:

1. Who owns the company?
2. Where does the labor come from?
3. Can you get the same people working on your files on a continuing basis?

4. Can you upload formats and letter-head for the service to use, or do you have to reformat and print on letter-head in your own office?
5. What is the normal turnaround time?
6. Does the company have support staff available 24/7/365?
7. What arrangements can you make to expedite turnaround time in an urgent situation?
8. What are the costs for normal and expedited turnaround?
9. What is the work quality? (You can get this information from references or by setting up a trial for yourself.)

I (Jeff) have used the services of LawDocs Express (www.lawdocsexpress.com) in the past and been very satisfied with it.

Send a Fax without a Fax Machine

The traditional office may have a dedicated fax machine or a multifunction fax/copier/ printer, but if you want to save money on installing a dedicated fax line, not to mention saving shelf space, you can turn your PC into a fax machine. Years ago, the fastest way to get a document into the hands of your opposing counsel or colleagues who were out of the office was to fax it. Today, you do better scanning a document as a PDF and e-mailing it.

Occasionally, though, some services (arguably archaic ones) communicate only via fax. Sometimes you will have clients who are more comfortable with a fax machine than with a scan and e-mail system. In any case, flexibility pays off, and you can easily set up a fax–to–e-mail/e-mail–to–fax system. If you find yourself in a bind, needing to send a fax from somewhere without an available fax machine, you can still send a fax as long as you have Internet access. Here are a few web-based fax services that can get your document out in pinch:

- Sfax
- Secure Fax by Innoport
- RingCentral
- MetroFax

When you choose an Internet fax service, you should expect some standard features:

- Customized cover pages
- Delivery notifications of faxes
- Fax logs

Let's take Sfax as an example. With this service, you can send an e-mail directly to a fax number, fax to multiple recipients, and receive e-mail notifications upon delivery of a fax. The online faxing service has auto resend should a fax fail to send, and also has mobile fax alerts. You can also get an option for international faxing on certain plans.

Most of these services work intuitively, and you can get started fairly easily. For example, with RingCentral, as with other services, you can send a fax via e-mail using the fax number (no "1") @rcfax.com, or you can send via the web, mobile, or desktop apps.

Ruby Receptionists

If you find yourself slowing down your practice as you transition into retirement, you may have less need to employ a full-time staff. Ruby Receptionists offers virtual phone receptionists to answer your calls and provide limited customer service for you. The receptionists answer your phone in a friendly and courteous manner, leaving your current and potential clients with the best impression, short of getting you on the first ring. Ruby's virtual receptionists answer your calls with a personalized greeting, including a friendly "Good morning/afternoon" or "Thank you for calling," along with your company name, and an offer of assistance. Although they have a standard greeting, they will customize how they answer according to your instructions You can also create scenario-specific instructions; for example, you can have messages from new clients forwarded to a specific line or e-mail. Going on vacation? You can instruct Ruby Receptionists to take messages from most clients and forward any calls from deadline-constrained client calls to you directly.

If you want, Ruby Receptionists can provide you with a toll-free number that you can publish on your website and marketing materials. If you cease to use the Ruby Receptionists service, you can take the toll-free number with you—no need to worry about having to update or reprint marketing materials.

Ruby Receptionists has staff available to answer the phone live from 7:00 a.m. to 8:00 p.m. Monday to Friday. These hours center around the typical business hours that your callers would expect a live person to answer your phone. Outside those times, Ruby can set up a variety of automated options, provided at no charge.

Ruby Receptionists may come off as pricey for a seemingly intangible service. Some folks may find it difficult to swallow paying for a receptionist that they do not actually see. The smallest package contains 100 minutes of receptionist time for $249 per month, 200 minutes for $409 per month, and 500 minutes for $819 per month. Ruby offers a free two-week trial for you to gauge approximately how many minutes you will use. On the other hand, compare those numbers to the cost of a full-time receptionist in your office.

If you decide to give Ruby Receptionists a try, we recommend you combine this service with a Google Voice, RingCentral, or similar service that enables you to route calls before they go through to the virtual receptionists. That way, clients whom you know to be frequent callers will not eat up your minutes.

Use Outlook's Follow-Up Reminder

When you create an e-mail in Outlook that requires a time-sensitive response, you can add a reminder to appear on your calendar, your recipient's calendar, or both. Creating a calendar reminder for yourself is a handy tool when you have a lot on your plate.

To set up an automatic reminder, first open a new e-mail message and create the e-mail as you normally would. Then locate the Follow Up menu on the Message tab. From the drop-down Follow Up menu, choose Custom. This allows you to create a custom reminder for yourself and/or your recipients. You can use this feature to create a monthly reminder to e-mail your clients with an update on their matter.

Amazon.com ... and Other Online Shopping Sites

The only thing better than window shopping is anytime anywhere desktop window shopping (and maybe a limitless credit card that somebody else pays off). Until the latter becomes available, anytime anywhere desktop window shopping is still pretty cool. With Amazon.com, you can find competitively priced technology (and other product) buys and have them shipped right to your door. Take advantage of the Amazon Prime Service, and you will find a variety of options with free second-day delivery. Amazon Prime allows you to scroll through reviews and product specifications for current models, and you can often find their older iterations through third-party vendors, if that is what you are looking for. The second-day delivery means you'll have your purchase in your hands often faster than you would if you planned to go to the store. How often have you told yourself, "I'll go pick that up this weekend," adding the item to the growing list of weekend stops to make before you can get to the point of relaxing? Do you remember the frustration you felt when you finally reached the store only to find out the one thing you came for was out of stock?

Here are some of the top reasons online shoppers look to Amazon:

1. **Price:** You can usually find better bargains on the website than in a brick and mortar store, although as with any store, you should scan all the options (including third-party vendors) for the best deal. On the bright side, you can adjust your search settings to have the lowest cost option appear first.

2. **Customer Service:** Amazon has pretty good customer service. When Amazon actually sells the product, they stand behind it. When a third party sells it through the Amazon site, it can get a bit dicey, but generally, Amazon will lean on the vendor to provide appropriate customer service. When you buy on Amazon, pay attention to whether Amazon acts as the seller or simply introduces you to the seller.

3. **Easy Returns:** We use the website regularly for buying tech accessories and have never had a problem returning merchandise if the purchase did not work or fit as advertised on the website.

Amazon's return policy is consumer friendly: you can return any new, unopened items sold and fulfilled by Amazon.com within 30 days of delivery for a full refund. Amazon will even cover the cost of shipping. If you are purchasing an item from a third-party vendor through Amazon.com, you need to read the return policy prior to ordering.

In addition to Amazon, you may want to point your browser to CDW, Newegg, and Tiger Direct for product and price comparisons for electronics products and accessories. You can shop around at four different stores during a single lunch hour without ever leaving your office.

Scan Your Way to Extra Space

While none of us want to think of our-selves as a hoarder, many of us store paper dating back for decades. Take a look at your home and office and think about how much space you can recover by getting rid of papers that you really do not need any longer.

Do you have closed files going back 15 or 20 or more years at your office? Do you pay a third party for storage space for those files? When did you last need to access any of them for anything? When do you think you will want or need to access them again? How much space do they take up? Can you think of anything better to do with the space?

At home, do you have bank and tax records going back well into the last cen-tury? How about a collection of instruction manuals for various devices that you have acquired (some of which you may not even have any longer)?

You get the picture. If you are like most of us, you have a lot of paper you do not need taking up a lot of space you could put to a more productive use. On the other hand, for whatever reason, you may not feel comfortable shedding all of those records and documents. How about making a compromise with yourself? Get a good scanner and start reducing the piles of paper to electronic files. You can store several rooms' full of paper files on a hard disk drive that you can fit in your coat pocket (feel free to get a larger hard drive if you prefer). A small investment of cash for the required equipment (assuming that you already have a computer, less than $600 for a couple of hard drives and a decent scanner) and some of your spare time can yield the following benefits:

1. Hard drives are a lot cheaper than the value of the space you will recover.
2. You can easily make backup copies of your files (without significant costs or using any noticeable amount of physical space).
3. You can get rid of the paper files, without losing the ability to refer to the records, should you ever figure out some reason to do so.

Scan Your Way to More Efficiency

Scanning works not only on old and unused files and documents, but also on your current files and documents in your home and at work. A good quality scanner lets you quickly scan client documents as they come into the office. Scanning a document takes no longer than copying it. In fact, you can get multipurpose scanner/copier/printer/fax machines that do all of those functions for you in the space of a single machine.

Similarly, at home, you can scan your current records as you get them and access them on your computer or tablet when you need them for tax preparation or whatever other purpose requires you to access them.

If you scan the records as you get them, at home or at work, you can store them more efficiently from the beginning. Scanning documents and accessing them on your computer makes it easier to locate them when you need them and makes it easier to take work with you on the road.

You get another major benefit from scanning your documents as you get them. Most of us have no system for backing up hard copies of documents. We have the records we store and that's the end of it. If a catastrophe occurs (fire, flood, hurricane, earthquake, and so on), we can lose our only copy of the documents. By storing them in electronic format, we can easily make a backup copy of them and keep it at a different location, thereby increasing the likelihood that we will not lose these documents to a single event.

What Scanner to Get?

To commence a life of scanning, you need to get a decent scanner. Scanners come in all sorts of configurations with a variety of features and at different price points. In deciding what to get, recognize that scanners come in three basic categories: (1) sheet-feed scanners, (2) flatbed scanners, and (3) hybrid scanners. A sheet-feed scanner scans only individual pages. A flatbed scanner scans individual pages or a bound book laid flat on the screen. A hybrid scanner can function both as a sheet-feed and a flatbed scanner. You can also get multifunction machines that scan, copy, print, and fax. Multifunction machines often have hybrid scanning capabilities.

For most uses, a sheet-fed scanner will prove the most efficient and cost effective. If you go that route, get a sheet-fed scanner that has an automatic document feed (ADF). ADF allows you to place a stack of documents on the scanner and let it automatically scan them. ADF for scanners comes in different capacities ranging from only a few sheets to a great many. Your need for higher or lower capacities will depend on your use.

You also should pay attention to the scanning speed (the rate at which the device can scan a page). Faster scanners cost more than slower ones.

If you want a good, reasonably fast, reliable, reasonably priced scanner, we have not found a better buy than the Fujitsu ScanSnap iX500. The scanner lists for $495, but you can find it online for about $420. The ScanSnap iX500 works with both the PC and Mac, providing an effective way to greatly reduce paper clutter at home and at work. It comes with the ability to scan wirelessly to a PC or Mac as well as iOS and Android mobile devices. You can get a detailed description of the scanner and its features on the Fujitsu website (www. fujitsu.com).

The Great Courses

Many of us have adopted a goal of lifelong learning either because we simply want to expand our horizons or because when it comes to our intellect, we have bought into the "use it or lose it" adage. We have many ways of approaching lifelong learning, ranging from attending courses at a local college or university, to attending other adult education courses, to taking online courses, to self-study. The Great Courses gives you another way to approach that goal. The Great Courses Company has recorded audio and/or video versions of college-level courses on a variety of subjects taught by some of the better educators from numerous colleges and universities. You can buy the courses and download audio and video files to your tablets or computers; you can have them ship you DVDs or CDs; or you can now access them from your computer or tablet and stream them. Be sure to go to the iTunes App Store or Google's Play Store and download the Great Courses app for your mobile device.

We have taken many courses this way and not yet found a bad one in the bunch. The available courses range from history to mathematics to philosophy to communication and also include many other categories. You can get the full list of available courses from the company's website at www.thegreatcourses.com.

The courses list for considerably less than you would pay for tuition to attend live at a college or university campus or even online. But the list price is misleading. Ever since we found out about The Great Courses and got on the mailing list, we have received regular print catalogs and e-mail solicitations about sales of their courses. The simple fact of the matter is that while a course may list for several hundred dollars, if you have a little patience, you can get it for a fraction of its list price. It appears that The Great Courses goes through an annual rotation in which it ultimately puts all of its courses on sale at various times in the year. If you wait for the course you want to go on sale, you might get it at a substantial discount (often as much as 70 percent off).

Check out the site and see what interests you. Try ordering a course to see how you like it. We predict you will order more going forward.

Cut the Cable!

Do you enjoy watching television? Do you get most of your television from the cable company or from a satellite distribution? If you use a satellite distribution, you have already cut the cable but not reaped many of the benefits derived from that, as you are still paying a lot of money to the satellite provider. What if we told you that you can cut the cable, still get most of the TV programs worth watching, and also cut your costs dramatically? Well, guess what! That is precisely what we are telling you!

You can get most of the classics, sports, and movies through the Internet. If you have a high-speed Internet connection and an Internet-ready (smart) TV, you have everything you need to get your programming online. If you do not have a smart TV, you can always get one (these TVs are not that expensive, and more and more sets are coming out Internet-ready). If you don't have a smart TV and do not want to rush out and buy one, then you can get a set-top Internet receiver from Roku or

Apple or Amazon, among others, that will make your TV just as smart as the next guy's. You can get premium programming through Internet-based subscriptions to media providers such as Netflix and HBO.

One additional tip: if you plan on going this way, you might want to kick up the speed of your Internet connection (usually available for a modest increase in the monthly provider charges). The cost of that increase and a few premium content subscriptions, plus the one-time charge for the receiver, should come out to a small fraction of the cost of similar programming through cable.

URL Shorteners

Uniform Resource Locators (or URLs for short) are specific character strings that serve as a sort of website mailing address, directing you to the specific location or web resource that you seek. As you can imagine with the number of web addresses and resources available today, the string can get rather long. Long URLs are more likely to get broken or copied wrong, so now various URL shortening services allow you to paste the full address into their system, and they will create a substantially shorter URL for you to copy into e-mails or presentations.

A good URL shortening service will also provide click-through information, valuable data to have when measuring the return on investment of your time spent posting or creating the presentations.

URL shorteners are particularly useful for social media marketing. Here are some popular URL shorteners:

- Tiny URL (www.tinyurl.com/)
- Bitly (https://bitly.com/)
- Google URL Shortener (https://goo.gl/)

Keep in mind that the system is not perfect. There are trade-offs to be made. Accessing a link through a URL shortener will take a little longer than if you clicked on the link directly as a result of the extra layer the link is navigating to get you to your destination.

Any.do

A user-friendly app for people on the go, Any.do may prove useful for keeping track of your to-do lists, whether it requires action today, tomorrow, or sometime in the future. Training yourself to use the app regularly allows you to clear your mind of all those little things you don't necessarily need to remember right away. With the app, you can create tasks, reminders, and to-dos all in one location.

You can also use Any.do as a handy list maker. Any.do has a unique feature called the Any.do moment that encourages making a habit of reviewing your daily tasks. You can manage your family and household to-dos along with your work and team projects.

For $3 per month (or $27 per year), you can subscribe to the premium version. The premium version lets you create recurring tasks and have an unlimited number of people collaborate on tasks. The free version allows collaboration, but restricts you to two users per task.

A web-based app also is available for Any.do, allowing people to use the service anywhere they have Internet access and can use a web browser.

The Pomodoro Technique®

The Pomodoro Technique® presents a time management method developed by Francesco Cirillo. Find yourself losing track of time or tasks taking longer than they should? Try this technique to refocus your attention. The technique involves breaking tasks into work intervals of 25 minutes each with short (5- to 10-minute) breaks in between each interval. The idea behind this technique is to maximize your focus while getting a project done and reduce the mental stress of interruptions.

The method is fairly simple. You work for 25 minutes and then take a 5-minute break. After four cycles of 25 minutes' work and a break of 5 minutes has passed, you then take a 15- to 20-minute break. The frequent breaks will help you stay focused, and knowing you will stop in a little while and have time to check e-mail or the Internet may make it easier to stay on task and finish a few things. Breaking up tasks into 25-minute intervals may make billing easier, too.

One of the benefits of this technique is that it is free; you can use any timer program on your computer or phone. If you go to the website at http://pomodorotechnique.com/, you can order your own pomodoro-shaped timer to use (if you find yourself in need of a kitchen timer, it can serve a dual purpose.)

The technique is not flawless, and it will not stop someone from barging in to your office to discuss an off-task item of business, nor will it prevent people from interrupting your brief break periods with work. But if it prompts you to finish items a little bit faster or helps break the distracting habits getting in your way, then it is worth a try, right?

Get Our Books

We think we may have saved the best tip for last (no cliché intended). We have written and continue to write books for lawyers to help them better understand, cope with, and benefit from technology. Because we consider ourselves among our favorite authors on technology and believe that you will find our books useful, we do not hesitate to recommend them to you.

Besides this book, we have three others already out: *Technology Solutions for Today's Lawyer* (American Bar Association GPSolo Division, 2013) *iPad for Lawyers* (West, 2013) and *Tech Tips* (American Bar Association GPSolo Division, 2016).

We have another book in process. It does not yet have an official title but it has a working title of *Technology for Litigators* (American Bar Association GPSolo Division).